CHINA AND CHRISTIANITY.

CHINA AND CHRISTIANITY

BY

ALEXANDER MICHIE

AUTHOR OF "MISSIONARIES IN CHINA"

BOSTON

KNIGHT AND MILLET

1900

Lane fund

F. H. Gilson Company
Printers and Bookbinders
Boston, U. S. A.

Introduction.

A few words of introduction to this volume may not be out of place, as the author and his writings are little known to American readers. Mr. Alexander Michie has been for nearly twenty years the correspondent of the London Times, resident in Peking. During that period he has enjoyed such advantages as come to the representative of so influential a journal. He has been brought into contact with not only the highest of Chinese official-dom, but with the representatives of foreign powers, many of whom have been prominent figures in the game of Diplomacy so actively played in the far East.

A careful observer, and a close student of all questions bearing upon the Chinese problem, he knows whereof he writes, and in this volume has discussed with rare calmness and sobriety the many perplexing questions which have culminated in the present deplorable outbreak in China.

This volume was published a few years since in Tien Tsin, reaching only a small circle of readers among the English speaking people of the East. Its merits entitle it to a wider reading, and there can be no more opportune occasion than the present to offer it to American readers, as a helpful aid to the formation of an enlightened public opinion on one of the burning questions of the hour.

THE PUBLISHERS.

PREFACE.

❦

A PUBLICATION which meets but qualified approval from esteemed friends may be thought to stand in need of an Apology.

There seems to be some fear that the tendency of the following essay is to widen rather than to heal the breach by fostering Chinese prejudice against Christianity on the one hand and displeasing an influential section of the foreign public on the other. Beneath this apprehension may possibly be a latent feeling that as regards the institutions of Christendom in the East, the rule for speakers and writers should be *nil nisi bonum*. But such implied immunity, if ever claimed in words, would not be conceded by one section of the Christian Church to another.

Fully recognizing that there is a time as well as a place to speak and to be silent, the writer

considers that the present is no time for reticence respecting matters which keep the relations between Chinese and foreigners in a state
of dangerous tension, but that on the contrary
it is just the time for plain speaking on these
burning questions. We Western nations stand
in a position of peculiar moral responsibility
towards China. She has not sought us, but
we her. She does not press her religion or
her polity on us, but we press ours on her.
In such a relationship the onus of justification
necessarily rests on the stronger who imposes
his will on the weaker; and where, as in the
present case, no competent neutral arbiter exists it becomes the duty of the aggressor himself, if he desires to be just, to assume, as far
as may be, the functions of such ideal referee,
and to give a patient consideration to all the
pleas, substantial or flimsy, advanced by, or on
behalf of, the weaker side.

This obligation, which has been understood
and loyally discharged in regard to such tangi-
ble matters as trade, carries tenfold weight
where moral relations are concerned; and those
who resolve to support religion, among an alien

people, by force, owe it to themselves to consider well both what they do, and how they do it. Errors in common affairs seldom sink so deep or spread so wide as to be irremediable, but mistakes in propagating and establishing religion may quickly pass beyond remedy, and bear consequences beyond calculation. For its transcendency involves misconception and misdirection; its purity gives the measure of its susceptibility to contamination; while its hold of the inner feelings of humanity diffuses and renders indelible whatever taint it may contract from its surroundings. Hence the tenacity of opinions and observances, even of a trivial character, which have once become incorporated with any religious cult. Hence also the difficulty of religious reform as compared with other kinds.

Obviously then an essence of such subtlety demands the finest tact on the part of those who have the handling of it, in whatever capacity. And though it is not possible, for want of a competent and acknowledged authority, to protect the Christianity as we guard the purity of the vaccine lymph which is imported into the country, it ought not to be too much to expect that the grosser elements of untruth, injustice and vulgar strife should be, as far as possible, eliminated alike from friendly and unfriendly association with the introduction into China of what is justly claimed to be the crown and consummation of the world's religions.

To those, if there be any such, who think the cause of religion may be served by hiding any part of the record it would be difficult to give an answer which is not already patent in the exceeding frankness of both the Hebrew and the Christian Scriptures. The fear of telling the Chinese too much would be in any case an idle fear, seeing the books of history and of observation lie wide open. Who, for example, shall prevent them from discussing the episode of Uganda? The recent dictum of an African missionary that "influence which is gained at the price of keeping unpleasant truths in the background is not worth having" has a wide application. No lasting understanding is likely to be attained between China and the Western world without unreserved communications touching matters of fact, and the dropping of all hypocritical pretences on both sides. No apology therefore ought to be necessary for even a perfunctory effort to expose misunderstanding, though it is at the same time devoutly to be wished that some competent hand, say, a missionary of light and leading, with experimental knowledge for his guide, may take up and develop the subject in a manner worthy of the great interests involved.

The issue at stake, in the conception of the writer, is nothing less than the mode in which Christianity shall be introduced to the largest population in the world; whether it shall enter in the gentleness of its true nature, like showers on thirsty soil; or with storm and cataclysm, leaving legacies of hate to future generations. Or rather such would have been the issue had matters not already gone beyond the bounds of so simple a formula. The question is now practically reduced to this, — whether the advance of Christianity shall approximate more to the one or the other of these alternative modes. Even in this attenuated form the subject is of serious import; for considering the flatness of the Chinese life

and the general poverty of its ideals the regen-
erating force of Christianity seems to be the
thing of which China stands most desperately
in need. "There is now in the world," says
Mr. Lilly in a recent work, "what we may
call the Christian temper, with all its charities
and courtesies, a temper of self-devotion to
some worthy cause, of self-effacement for some
high end, of fortitude and forgiveness, of
purity and pitifulness, of generosity and gentleness." If to bring the Chinese within the influence of such a "temper" be an object
worthy of all sacrifice, it behoves those concerned to see to it that the very considerable
sacrifices — in money and in precious lives, in
political principle and in international comity
— which are now being made be not operating
as hindrances to the desired process.

Needless to say it is beside the author's
purpose to discuss Christianity in any way
whatsoever. Only the vehicles and wrappage
of it are touched on, and these no further than
seemed necessary to clear the ground for the
political survey. The theme is not "China"
nor "Christianity," still less the two combined,

but only the thin ragged line of actual or potential contact between them, external to both. So much, and no more of the colliding surfaces is glanced at as was requisite for a superficial diagnosis of the collision. It will be for the courteous reader, who may deem it worth while, to judge whether the prescribed limit has been overstepped.

The motive of the essay is to draw attention to the breach of continuity between the minds of the several high contracting parties under whose combined authority the propagation of Christianity is carried on in China, and to suggest the want of a more harmonious adjustment between the parts of a complex politico-religious machine made up of heterogeneous elements. The present is a natural sequel to the tract on "Missionaries in China" published last year. In that essay the prominence was given to the methods of the propaganda; in this the broader considerations which affect the policy of governments and administrative bodies are more particularly dwelt upon. The subjects overlap to a certain extent, but repetitions have been as much as possible avoided. The notes, somewhat promiscuously thrown in while the sheets were in the press, have been culled, with scarcely an exception, from casual readings after the text was written; and they thus possess, for the author at least, a certain corroborative and corrective value.

No one can be more sensible than the author of the lame and the almost negative conclusion to which his meandering excursion has inevitably led. The fiction of looking through the glasses of a *fin-de-siècle* Chinese politician is clumsy and halting, and perhaps this attempt to " see ourselves as others see us " attains no nearer to a true presentment of the reality than those school-room diagrams which profess to show how the Earth looks as viewed from the Moon. But it possesses this advantage over them that it can be tested and its blemishes exposed.

A. M.

CONTENTS.

China and Christianity.

✄ ✄ ✄

I.

STATE PROBLEMS AND THE CHINESE WAY OF SOLVING THEM.

In common with all other states China has to grapple with the two problems of internal polity and external relations; but she treats them with a patience and a passiveness peculiarly her own, which has constantly to be borne in mind in estimating the motives of her action in any given circumstances. Foreign precedents have little or no weight with China, and hers are for the most part as far removed from European conventional ways as the East is distant from the West. It is, however, the misfortune of the Chinese Government and people to be weighed in a balance which they have never accepted; and to have their short-

comings, so ascertained, made the basis of re-
clamations of varying degrees of gravity.
Naturally, therefore, the bill of grievances from
time to time presented by foreign nations fails
to reach the conscience of China, just as the
unwearied criticisms from without on her ne-
glect of good government fall absolutely dead.
The want of the receptive faculty renders the
result of all such representations as blank as
a photograph on an unprepared plate.

In the case of her external relations, however, force may be and has been used to supply
the lack of reasoned conviction, and a me-
chanical compliance with Western practices,
within narrow limits, thereby more or less established. But so far as it is against nature,
so far is such conformity liable to break down
unless the machinery which produced it is kept
in constant motion.

In their academical discussions foreigners
usually take the fullest cognizance of this state
of things, and those of them who do not come
into direct contact with the Chinese are perhaps disposed to make even undue allowance
for the hardships of their position. Those, on

the other hand, who are placed at the points of international collision are in the habit of insisting on the Chinese people and government being measured absolutely by Western .standards as the only condition under which working relations can be maintained. Indeed, the pioneers of commerce and Christianity, strung up to a high pitch of zeal for the success of their respective schemes, require the Chinese to submit, in strict accordance with treaty of course, to demands which could not even be named to any other sovereign State. And they seem to expect not only immediate compliance, but cheerful and hearty compliance. Dr. Griffith John, for example, in his able statements of the missionary case, makes a special grievance of the want of alacrity which the Chinese show in obeying the behests of foreign powers. Though knowing full well that he and his cause are only maintained in China by external force overruling the settled policy of the Government, based on the interests of the lettered class and the convictions of the people, he nevertheless, in his communications to the papers in China and England,

makes it a serious part of his accusation of the
Chinese Government that the foreign Ministers
had to complain of the great difficulty with
which they obtained the promulgation of the
Imperial Edict condemning the populace for
their attacks on missionaries in 1891.   Let the
case be imagined of an alien propaganda in
Kazan or Kieff being set upon by a posse of
popes and ruffians, and then reflect on the kind
of "difficulty" a German or English Minister
would experience in obtaining the publication
of an Ukase condemning wholesale the assailants and lauding the strangers as immaculate!
Though China must be held to her engagements, there always will be a difference between the manner of fulfilment of a voluntary
obligation and of compliance with one imposed
by force, especially if it runs counter to national feeling; and there is wisdom in frankly
recognizing what cannot in any case be disputed
or altered.[1]

[1] The despatches of the British Minister published in the
Riots Blue Book, 1892, and the press criticisms thereon, are
pitched in the same tone of astonishment at the reluctance and
insincerity of the Chinese — as if these were quite new discoveries!

Perhaps, however, all these pioneers are right, for life to each one of them is too short to wait for the Chinese mind to be educated up to the point of willing assent to their various aggressive pretensions; and too short for them even to attempt to comprehend the Chinese way of looking at things. Hence, with them, "force," in its most direct form, is the only "remedy" within reach. While, however, admitting that such may be the only safe and practical ground which the advanced guards of foreigners can wisely take up, in the actual circumstances, there is behind and around them, though aloof from the heat and dust of the struggle, a whole atmosphere of opinion of varying density in which ideas are generated as clouds are formed in the clefts of the mountains, and where influences slowly gather which eventually shape the ends of the toilers in the valleys, rough hew them how they may. Such phenomena, merely to take two current instances, as the anti-opium and the Indian factory labour agitations which are fermenting in England, and seemingly gaining force, without reference to the interests or opinions of the

parties directly concerned, may serve to re-
mind all classes of men who are too much
absorbed in their own calling to give full
consideration to aught but the exigencies of
the day, that, independently of them, there
may be latent forces eventually capable of
over-ruling them in unforeseen ways, for good
or evil.

The principle on which the Government of
China regulates its national affairs, internal and
external, is, as has been hinted, that of mas-
terly inactivity. Chinese statesmen and place-
hunters do not find congenial occupation in
remodelling the constitution, as is the case in
some other countries, but rather acquiesce in the
distempers of the body politic like an easy-going
man who never seeks the aid of a physician.
Everything is left to nature, and when matters
go wrong they are usually allowed to right
themselves as best they may. Hence the
Chinese — for people and Government are the
same — are seen to suffer abuses of every kind
to consume their substance with the same fatal-
istic apathy with which they meet natural
calamities. They recoil from political experi-

mentation, and oppose to all innovations an immense silent resistance, especially in cases where they cannot form a distinct conception of the real scope or tendency of the change.

II.

FOREIGN RELATIONS.

IT is the same patient imperturbable spirit which directs the foreign policy of China. She makes no plunges, but advances, when forced, by tentative and reluctant steps, with the skid on every wheel. Her constitution, the out-come of the empiricism of many ages, and her natural temperament, of which it is the em-bodied expression, combine in a harmony of slow movements, and excessive deliberation. So consistently, indeed, does this characteristic dominate governmental action that the dilatory precautions which are taken to meet impending changes not only fail to overtake the object, but through their untimeliness, actually create new and gratuitous dangers.

It is only on some such theory as this that the confused and irritating position of her foreign relations seems explicable. The West-ern nations did not give China the time necessary for her to think, but rushed her into action for which she was unprepared, which she did not understand, and for which she has to suffer whatever may be the consequences of the blind bargain she was compelled to make.

Had the Government of China been fully acquainted with the character of the Western nations it would perhaps have run all risks to exclude them from the territory, absolutely and forever. Not even the modicum of a strangled commerce such as that carried on at Macao and Canton, nor the Russian prisoners entertained, with their priests and teachers, for 200 years in Peking, nor the coquetting with the Catholic missionaries during the sixteenth and seventeenth, and even the later centuries, would have been permitted. Only by complete seclusion could China hope to remain what she had been, or even to secure her stability as a united and homogeneous nation. But having small conception of either the power or the spirit of the Christian nations, and like statesmen all over the world, dealing from hand to mouth with the circumstances of the day, the rulers of China admitted the foreigner in the North

and the South, in his threefold character —
political, commercial, and religious.

There are intuitions which precede knowledge; and as the instincts of certain animals
enable them, even without experience, to recognize the hereditary enemies of their race, so
the advent of foreigners seems to have inspired
the Chinese with a certain indefinable fear,
begotten perhaps of their traditional experience
in dealing with their territorial neighbours.
But the strangers were so insignificant and so
deferential that curiosity overcame caution, and
transitory obscured permanent interests, and so
it came about that instead of shutting them
out of the country the Emperors were content
to place the foreigners under close surveillance.
The fate of their empire was probably in a
certain sense as much sealed by those innocent
admissions as was that of the Ottoman empire
in Europe by the first capture of Azoff by the
Czar of Muscovy in 1696, though in both
cases the process of disintegration may be indefi-
nitely protracted.　Only a small leak through
the reservoir, it is true, but a fissure ever widen-
ing, and with the pressure of incumbent water

ever increasing, certain to end in bringing down
the whole flood on the valley below, either in
the form of devastating torrents or in safe and
beneficent streams, as fate and the nature of
the preparations for its reception may determine. The regulation of the inflow has hitherto
proved too much for the Chinese. Perceiving
the potency of the new force, they dreamed of
schemes of expulsion so ill conceived that each
step taken to repress the foreign invasion invariably resulted in opening new avenues for
its advance, every concession made to the
foreigner serving but to stimulate his appetite
for more.

The actual situation resulting from this des-
ultory contest is naturally regarded with different eyes by the various parties concerned.
There are doubtless foreigners who would
anticipate even the break-up of the empire
with the kind of weird glee with which wanton
boys hail conflagrations, and some who, while
they would sincerely deplore such a catastrophe, would still think even that price not
too dear to pay for the progress and enlightenment of the people who would survive the dis-

I

solution of the empire, and who represent the ultimate interests to be served. Among the Chinese themselves, too, diversities of senti- ment on the subject of imperial unity and per- manence may easily be credited. But the government, the governing classes, both pres- ent and future, have the one burden laid upon them, by the meanest as well as by the noblest considerations that can rule the actions of men, of preserving the empire, the dynasty, and the existing polity intact as they have received them; and should that come to be visibly hopeless, then at least to make as long a fight in their defence as possible. Among patriotic statesmen animated by this common aim, there will of course still be divisions according to mental calibre and natural temperament, quite sufficient, under given conditions, to dislocate the machinery of government and reduce it to impotency. Some would resist not invasion merely, but all innovation, as such, and would defend the old *régime* in all its parts with their last breath; while others would encourage even sweeping reforms in order thereby to gain strength to resist effectually what may be found resistible. By a miracle of regeneration, of which, however, not the faintest symptom is yet apparent, the threatening danger might be averted, and a true reforming party in the country might thus render to the State the most essential service.

But whatever differences may divide them as to their methods, all parties probably unite in the aim of conserving the State from every change imposed on it from without, whether by the direct force of arms or by the spread of the subtler though not less potent social forces. It is incumbent, therefore, on those who are responsible for the peace and honour of the Chinese empire, before all things to acquaint themselves accurately with the nature of the complex foreign forces which are pressing on it from every side.

III.

FOREIGN RELIGION.

OF all the elements of which the invading force is made up none is more formidable than the religious element, from which the ultimate danger to the political fabric is the most likely to arise. Already the religion of the foreigners has shown itself fearlessly aggressive, and it possesses faculties of expansion and intensity which, if allowed free play, may in no long time cause the religious to tower over all the other foreign interests in the demands which it will make on Chinese hospitality. The relations of the government to the foreign religion, or religions, are so far simplified that there can henceforth be no question of excluding them, as they are already established in fact, and protected in law, by treaty. What remains for the Chinese government to consider is how to deal with these religions so as to get out of them the greatest amount of good, and to minimize the evils incidental to their propagation. For which purpose as careful a study as the circumstances permit should be made of the religious system which is forcing itself without ceremony wherever it can find an opening throughout the empire.

The international credentials of Christianity, as registered in the various treaties of 1858 on which toleration was stipulated for its teachers and followers, are simple in the extreme: it inculcated virtue and taught men to do as they would be done by. But the Chinese had their own experience of the inadequacy of this description, which, moreover, would be rejected as insufficient by most Christians; and it is perhaps to be regretted that the foreign negotiators, who were solely responsible for the phraseology, should have condescended to apologetic expressions, since the treaties were made in their hour of victory. The partiality of the description was not calculated to remove prejudice from the Chinese mind as to the merits of the religion, a prejudice which would naturally operate with renewed force as soon as the grip of the soldier was relaxed. Perhaps,

however, this is of little importance now that
the statesmen of China are called upon to form
their opinion of the Christian religion from
fresh data, and to judge therefrom of the character of the protection to which it may be entitled. On one side the representatives of
Christianity challenge examination of what they
promulgate, and on the other the exigencies of
the State demand that the challenge be taken
up by the public men of China; and they will
evade it at their own peril and that of the
common weal.

But what must be the embarrassment of a
Chinese statesman who approaches this inquiry
in a serious spirit? If he asks — what and
where is Christianity? the first answer will be
a babel of conflicting, nay, mutually destructive
claims from a hundred different quarters, each
claimant calling aloud, Lo, it is here! Close
attention to their utterances would show him
that a doctor of Christianity can hardly deliver
himself of an exegesis, however chiselled and
chastened, but some other teacher of equal
eminence will promptly assail it. It might
perhaps occur to a laborious-minded heathen

to try to discover Christianity by the exhaustive process of placing the contradictions of its rival exponents [1] over against each other, and by cancelling out all the propositions which were at variance, attain at last to the unchallengeable quintessence. But the residuum, though in reality vital, would, to the apprehension of such a man, be so intangible as to suggest doubt of the accuracy of the analysis. If, dazed by the discords of its miscellaneous professors, he should think of harking back to the fountain-head with the view of seeking to understand Christianity by searching the rec-

---

[1] " How much harm has been done by the jealousy and enmity between Lutherans and Calvinists in the time of the Reformation in Germany, between Episcopalians and Dissenters in England, and in our mission work in China by the term-question controversy, and the separation caused by it. Human passion and sin, sometimes misnamed ' conscience,' lies beneath all these eruptions of human nature." — DR. FABER.

" Protestantism is not only a veritable Babel but a horrible theory, and an immoral practice which blasphemes God, degrades man, and endangers Society."—CARDINAL CUESTA'S Catechism (1872), cited by Prof. SCHAFF.

" DR. ELDER CUMMING of Glasgow draws attention to the great evils of the day, and especially to the prevalent indifference to the growth of the Romish Church."—Messenger, April, 1892.

problem in the true sense of the word that presses on China, but a politico-eeclesiastical question; the alleged rights of societies of men who, having adopted certain religious tenets, base thereon their claim to special civil privileges. That is a clear deduction alike from historical records and contemporary observation.

It is not uncommon, and it is moreover perfectly fair, for Christian propagandists to claim modern Europe as voucher for the merits of their religion; although it may appear to be bringing forward the strength and magnificence of the kingdoms of the earth to attest the power of the kingdom emphatically declared to be " not of this world." It is, however, a plea better calculated to confirm the allegiance of adherents than to carry complete conviction to the mind of an unsympathetic spectator. Our imaginary Chinese inquirer, for example, might ask, as others have done, whether blue eyes and red hair have not somewhat to do with the progress of Europe; whether Christianity be not in its full development as much the consequence as the cause of Western civilization, the two reacting on each other. And he might even allege drawbacks to the perfection of European society, as certain Chinese in fact have done, not without a superficial show of success. The elevation of women, to select the commonest item in the list of the social triumphs of Christianity, — which, however, it may be contended, is an achievement not wholly Christian, but partly Teutonic — while it has conferred immeasurable benefits on society, has not been obtained without the payment of a price, as every newspaper and novel of the day testify.

The morality of trade supplies a more generally intelligible — though in fact a quite fallacious — test, and on that ground we have it on the authority of the manager of a great Banking Corporation that the Chinese stand well. In other departments of life they fall decidedly short of at least the modern standards of Christendom, as for instance in the barbarity of their practices in war, and in judicial proceedings.

The radical difference, however, between the

Christian and non-Christian people of the
world shows itself rather in the progressive
vigour of the one as contrasted with the dull
and languorous resignation of the other ; and
this is a distinction which is visible at first
sight.   A learned Oriental, not Chinese nor
Christian, once remarked to the writer that the
immense difference between Buddhism and
Christianity might be seen in the streets of
Peking as compared with those of Paris.   Nor
is it on the mere passive virtues that any
advocate would rest the superiority of the
Christian over all other systems, but rather on
the energy of its positive philanthropy and
the principle of self-sacrifice which drives the
vast benevolent machinery of Christian countries, and to which there is nothing at all corresponding in the non-Christian world.   This
could hardly escape any candid observer of
facts.[1]

[1] "More than once I have heard a patient say, 'There is
no such love as this in all China.'"— *China Med. Journal.*

Organized philanthropy all over the world is, for the most
part, directly connected with active Christianity; and in all
schemes of help for the Chinese, as in schools, hospitals, famine
relief, it is the Christian missionaries who prompt the movement
and who alone can be relied upon for any sustained effort.

The manifest strength of the Western nations is, however, calculated to make a deeper impression on the mind of an average Oriental than their moral superiority. And China, at its wit's end to find means of defending itself, would doubtless accept Christianity with eagerness if it were but persuaded that strength was a transferable commodity which would be imported with the religion. But to import that which nourishes strength is not necessarily to acquire strength. Much depends on the powers of assimilation which, until proved, must remain uncertain, and can, in this case, only be proved by experiments which bar retreat. It is with religion as with material civilization, the form without the spirit would be a dead and useless thing, of which the present condition of the new Chinese navy may be cited as a case in point.

But without accepting in full the proposition sometimes offered, in good faith, to China that she would become strong by becoming Christian, Chinese statesmen will nevertheless do well to trace the steps by which the nations of the West have attained to their present emi-

nence in arts and arms, and they will certainly
derive advantage from the study of the long
and sanguinary struggles by which the various
States have carved their way through barbarism
like African explorers cutting tracks through
the dark forest into the open light.

IV. ,

EXOTERIC CHRISTIANITY.

THE conditions under which Christianity first made its way in the Western world naturally suggest comparison with its present relations to China. The analogy between the old empire of Rome, and the existing Chinese empire is, indeed, obvious, but the circumstances determining the attitude of the respective States towards the Christian system are so discrepant that unless the qualification " exceptions excepted " be kept constantly in mind misleading inferences may easily be drawn from it. Rome made the acquaintance of Christianity as an infant of unsuspected potentialities; China encounters a full grown giant with a long dramatic history. Such a contrast puts parallelism out of the question; while that decisive new factor, the support of the modern propaganda by some half-dozen of the greatest military powers, almost invalidates comparison between the condition of the modern Church and that of the friendless followers of Him whose kingdom was not of this world.

The most definite impression which the progress of Christianity in the early centuries of its growth would be likely to make on a quite disinterested mind would probably be that of the radical strength of a movement which, through the faith and fervour of its adherents, had proved itself irresistible; an impression not altogether reassuring as to the political fate of nations on whom such a heavy stone might fall. The Christians, while yet a feeble band, would be seen stretching out their hands to grasp at power, and by sheer force of will and cohesion actually obtaining it, and gradually gaining control of the affairs of the State. The Christian subjects of the empire of the world would be observed indifferent to its decline, and if not actively accelerating, at least doing little to arrest its fall, and eventually entering on possession of the escheated estate, being the only capable men. One practical deduction which a Chinaman might draw from these events would be that the old bottles were hardly good enough to hold such strong wine; and another, that if, at the end of 1900 years, Christianity can boast of her social triumphs, they have been gained at the cost of the philosophies and civilization which previously existed.[1]   Reflections of this kind may well suffice to put the statesmen of an empire as yet unchristianized on their guard in face of so great a force, and to stir them to deep inquiry into its nature, aims, and methods.   They are not, however, called upon to weigh the remote results of Christianity; for the immediate present and the near future more than tax the statesman's capacity for practical excogitation; nor has he any mission beyond his own State.   The ultimate good of the human race is no concern of his; and mankind at large will do better without his gratuitous solicitude.

It would be interesting to know the musings of a Chinese Emperor who could place himself in imagination in the shoes of one of the Cæsars of the first or second centuries.

[1] "The most serious trouble for Japan at present is the extinction which has necessarily befallen her old code of morals and ethics in the presence of the new civilization."—*Japan Mail.*

Could they have foreseen the future how would they have demeaned themselves towards the nascent religion ? It is permissible to suppose that if the Antonines had really understood Christianity they must have yielded personally to its claims, and yet, had its future course been revealed to them, they must, in duty to the empire as an emperor would regard it, have extinguished it as a society. Could a sincere Christian then persecute the Christian Church ? It would be a paradox, perhaps, but scarcely a contradiction, for between personal religion and the pretensions of an ambitious corporation there is the clearest distinction. And was not the history of the Church for many centuries the unfolding of continuous divergence from the precepts and the practices of its Founder, who nevertheless in some fashion or other retained and retains the allegiance of all sections of the universal Church ? Here in fact is the difficult question : how the mixed bodies of self-styled Christians, such as we see them in the world to-day, make good their title to the name.

Between the spirituality of the religion of

Christ, its elevating, purifying, and vivifying power over individual men — in other words, between the personal piety of Christians — and the assumptions of collective Christianity, there is a gulf as wide as the world. Whether happily or unhappily, the two have been so joined together that no man can now sunder them ; and they must in practice be treated as one. It is with Christians as with political and other combinations : the individual character of the members is subdued to the interests, or dogmas, or principles of the whole body. Taken separately they may be modest, truthful, and charitable, while collectively they may be constrained to approve actions of an opposite kind such as individually they would condemn. Though, therefore, Christians, like other men, invariably — and quite naturally — put forward their innocent side as their title to consideration, it must be repeated that that is not the only side which rulers of States have to take account of. Personal piety, charity, and self-sacrifice are in truth qualities too subtle to be weighed in the coarse scales of the politician, who can only, even in Christian — how much

more in non-Christian—countries deal with
the external manifestations of Christian societies as they collide and interact with the other
elements of the body politic.   It is with them
as with the dual character of the private citizen.
The law, or the State, deals with the several
members of society not according to their in-
nate worth or purity of motive, but strictly
according to their public record; and the man
of exemplary life, the pious son, devoted hus-
band, and loving father who levies ship-money
or moves his neighbour's landmark is not
allowed to plead in defence the fine qualities
of his personal morality.   As Christian critics
of Mohammedanism usually brush away the
religious emotions which give it life, so must
politicians, as such, virtually set aside the ethe-
real principle which animates Christianity,
more especially politicians who are themselves
heathen.

The attention of an intelligent Chinese inquirer would naturally be drawn to the different
aspects which Christianity has assumed in the
successive stages of its growth, and throughout
the wide regions where it has taken root; its

chronological and its ethnical developments.
The intangible abstraction, pure Christianity,
he could only hope to deduce from many and
various *data*, as the ideal focus of some great
ellipse may be inferred from observations at
different points of its circumference. Everywhere he would see the characteristic products
of the human nature of the people compounded
with the forms of the religion which they have
severally adopted. Of extant Christianity the
mere geographical distribution will perhaps
suggest as much as is necessary respecting the
main features of these compounds, without elaborate description. Its manifestations in Northern and Southern Europe and America, in
Russia, Switzerland, and Abyssinia may serve
as types of generic varieties; while that colos-
sal compendium, the Church of Rome, contains
within itself almost every colour which the
many-coloured mind of man has imparted to
his religion.

The observer of this vast panorama spread
out over the Western world is naturally
prompted to compare these diverse forms, and
to deduce, if it be possible, from the visible

results the causes of their differentiation, as
well as the secret of their harmony, so far as
harmony may be discoverable.   The complex
influence of climate, soil, and worldly circumstances, modes of life, of race, of education, of
political history, of communications, of epochs,
of the personality of apostles, of authority, of
wars, of hardships, of luxury; in a word of
the myriad formative agencies which combine
to build up the character of humanity — might
suggest to one who came fresh to the subject
the attempt to render some rational account of
the varied development of popular Christianity, and to unravel the double mystery of its
catholicity and its narrowness.   For him, however, who is only in quest of such light as will
guide him in the despatch of business within
his own province, such an exhaustive investigation, probably impossible even for a Buckle,
would be quite out of place.   He will have to
content himself with bold and rapid generaliza-
tions, fortunate if these may perchance help
him to forecast in some vague manner the
character which the religion of Christ might be
expected to assume, when transplanted to the

soil of China. For that is the real point on which the interest of the inquest converges.

Inasmuch, however, as contemporary Christian nations are so far removed in race, traditions, and civilization from the actual condition of the Chinese State, the comparative study of these co-existing societies would yield, at the best, results too speculative for use, and it would be necessary, at the very least, to supplement it by a chronological review of the descent of modern Christianity, through its many channels, from its origin. And this would be the simpler undertaking of the two in that the materials of such a review have already been digested by historical students who, if not impartial, are at least sufficiently distant from the events they describe to form a judgment clearer than it is possible for an ordinary man to form with respect to the transactions of his own time. The modern world indeed, whether social, political, or religious, would be as unintelligible without some knowledge of the successive agitations which have produced it as words often are without their etymology; and on the other hand past events

would be very imperfectly understood without
the retrospective light thrown on them by the
consummations to which they have in their
different ways led up.   Every stage of its progress will reveal something of the true nature
of Christianity, fragmentary, however, like the
tesselæ of a mosaic picture, and whosoever
would gain an approximately just idea of it
must take it in perspective, looking at the beginning from the end, and at the end from the
beginning.

From the time when the movement gathered
its new-born forces timidly and anxiously in
an upper room in Jerusalem to the ubiquitous
display, courageous and confident, of our own
day, the drama of Christianity has never
ceased to be crowded with incidents which
stand out and challenge investigation.   Like a
stream from the mountains cutting its way im-
partially through all obstructions the new
religion burst through every class and condition of men : the remnants of the philosophers
of Greece, the soldiers and politicians of Rome,
Arabs on one side and Goths on the other,
the commonest and rudest barbarians as well as

the most cultured scholars, reducing them all
to the common level of subjects of the Church;
and all the chords of human life were agitated
to the uttermost.

In its passage through so many strata the
stream was perhaps enriched rather than puri-
fied, for the *débris* of the different paganisms
which it undermined was borne on its bosom
and distributed over the new continent of unfolding thought like the glacial boulders which
are strewn over Europe, far from the rock
bed whence they were detached. And even as
scientists speculate as to the origin of the one
so do metaphysicians find their ingenuity sometimes taxed to trace the genealogy of the
other. During its long and chequered course,
the Church has shown itself in depression
and in triumph, in the extremes of poverty
and of wealth, and almost in the extremes of
depravity and virtuous exaltation, and it has
shown how the principles of Christianity re-act
on many varieties of race and character and
many phases of human life. The history of
the Church is thus a museum of vital experiments worked out but not yet fully classified,

an open book from which no hungry mind, whether learned or unlearned, need turn empty away.

The question then is: What leading impressions of Christianity would a moderately informed Chinese be likely to derive from such a hurried survey of the past and present as is above suggested, and what conception might he form of the probable social results of its inoculation into the actual life of China? No man not himself in contact with the magnetic power of Christianity can hope to appreciate its value in the regeneration of individual character; and it is scarcely necessary to repeat that the spiritual or essential element which has kept Christianity from breaking up is necessarily left out of account, the superficial or political aspect of it being alone here considered.

With these important eliminations, then, the salient features of Christianity most likely to arrest the attention of the supposed inquirer may be surmised to be something like the following:

(1.) He would be impressed with the vitality of a system which has succumbed neither to external opposition nor to its own follies and crimes, though he would not fail at the same time to note certain significant exceptions to its success in the debased Christianity of Africa, Arabia, and Syria, which disappeared before the sweep of the more vigorous Islam. Indeed, the struggle which was carried on with fluctuating fortune for many centuries between the low types of Christianity and the virile creed and government of Mohammed would not be the least interesting portion of the survey, seeing that, as has happened in India, China will have to accommodate both competitors.

(2.) The next characteristic of Christianity which would interest the inquirer would perhaps be its undeviating progressiveness, its intolerance,[1] its love of power,[2] and its tacit or explicit assumption of infallibility.

[1] A diplomatic Secretary of Pope Pius VII. declared that it was " of the essence of the Catholic religion to be intolerant."

[2] Not an ignoble desire. Ruskin says *à propos* of some reflections of Dean Milman: " You may observe, as an almost unexceptional character in the ' sagacious wisdom ' of the Protestant clerical mind, that it instinctively assumes the desire of

In the infancy of the movement, when the Christians had as yet scarce ventured to show themselves out of doors, they would be seen assuming authority over their neighbours. And the spirit of governing so runs through the veins of the Christian body, even to the small capillaries, that there is hardly a village in Christendom but those of its inhabitants who appropriate to themselves in a special sense the name of Christian would be found in one way or another trying to rule their neighbours. Strife being so natural to man it would be absurd to charge Christianity with all the wars which have convulsed Christendom. It is nevertheless true that religion imparts an energy to quarrels, whether on the great or the small stage, such as commoner motives fail to do; and also that a large proportion of the great wars of Christendom have been avowedly religious in their origin and aim. Nor does dismemberment quench the spirit of

power and place not only to be universal in Priesthood, but to be always *purely selfish* in the ground of it. The idea that power might possibly be desired for the sake of its benevolent use, so far as I remember, does not once occur in the pages of any ecclesiastical historian of recent date."

the Church, for like the annelids which propagate by fission, each offshoot reproduces integrally the attributes of the parent, and the least of them is ready to stand up before the world and defend, with whatever weapons[1] happen to be available, its claim to rule by divine right over its neighbours. Every sect is thus in its nature a potential persecutor,[2] as indeed all religions are, and the long struggles for "religious liberty" have usually been for liberty to control others,[3] fortunately tempered in its action in modern days by the superior efficiency of civil government. Perhaps after all, this is no more than to say that the Christian sects are full of life.

But what a paradoxical spirit it is! Diffident in matters of daily experience; puzzled

---

[1] " Flogging, branding, and other agreeable forms of recrimination were familiar enough as from Puritan to Quaker." — *Saturday Review*, 12th March, 1892.

[2] " Even the reformers were as furious against contumacious errors as they were loud in asserting the liberty of conscience. . . . The Puritans in turn became persecutors when they got the upper hand (1645)."— JUSTICE DUNCAN, cited by Professor SCHAFF.

[3] " The cry for religious equality means the desire for irreligious persecution." — *Ibid.*, 16th January, 1892.

by the commonest phenomena; unable to foresee the issue of the simplest combination; failing wherever their judgment can be brought to any practical test; many professors of Christianity nevertheless, in matters which eye hath not seen nor ear heard, "most ignorant of what they're most assured," assume a position of certainty so absolute as to warrant them in employing all the forces at their command to compel other men to their opinion. And whenever they find it feasible they aspire to attach the civil government itself to their particular service. Governments everywhere have as much as they can do to guard their machinery from being used by the sects for purposes of coercion, the instinct for which seems to be irrepressible. Nor indeed could it be logically otherwise so long as each sect believes from its heart that it is really entrusted with the oracles of God.

It need not surprise the student that in the origin of Christianity no countenance was given to pretensions to domination, [1] while the con-

---

[1] "There is nothing whatever in the doings and teachings of our Lord which could be used to justify religious intolerance and persecution." — DR. FABER.

trary principle was laid down as fundamental.
For no system, whether of religion or philos-
ophy, is able long to maintain its pristine
purity. All known religions have diverged
widely from the precepts and practices of their
founders, Islam perhaps the least of all. The
collective militant temper, however, is, fortunately, not inconsistent with personal kindliness, according to the law of human nature
before alluded to under which men are willing
to serve their corporations by means which
they would scruple to use for their personal
interests. Hence the frequent observation that
certain persons are " better than their creed."
The rule applies also, conversely, to those
whose moral standards belong to an inferior
order, who seek their own advantage by means
which they would not resort to for the common good.

(3.) Growing naturally out of the preceding
conditions is the compact formation of " the
Church " in its many varieties, whose solidarity
gives energy, and which is the immediate
cause of religious persecution, whether by
Christians or of Christians.

It might have been supposed *a priori* that essential Christianity, the devotion of individuals to the person of Christ (to take a short but inadequate definition), needed no such formal combination of men, and that vital religion would even be overlain to extinction by the pomp and circumstance, to say nothing of the coarser matters, inseparable from large organizations. But as a common loyalty to Christ implies the brotherhood of man, of which the various Christian societies may be taken as separate nuclei, destined eventually to coalesce, the principle of association must be recognized as fundamental with them. When the followers of Christ began to call themselves " brethren " the Church was already formed ; and there it stands to-day, the grain of seed grown into a wide-spreading tree with many branches, and its roots struck deep into the soil of humanity ; the visible embodiment of Christianity.

(4.) A necessary development of the cohesive quality of the Church was its self-governing tendency, which declared itself in its earliest days and has grown with the growth of Christianity.

But a section of any national community separated in aims, sympathy, and organization from the rest must be a source of jealousy even to strong governments, and an occasion of alarm to weak ones. And even in cases where the weakness of government may itself be pleaded in justification of separate autonomies, which claim to fulfil, though in an irregular manner, the functions of a national government, that is the last plea likely to be admitted by incapable rulers. The Roman Emperors looked askance at all associations not recognized by and subordinate to the public law, and the Church of Rome, though itself the sublimest example ever known of an *imperium in imperio*, has never even to the present day been able to extend its toleration to the harmless mysteries of the Freemasons. The Christian Church, indeed, has in all ages been the most indigestible morsel in the form of an empire within the empire that ever existed excepting where, as in Russia, it has been incorporated whole into the scheme of State

government; for to its vigour and self-asser-
tion, and its claim to be a law to itself it added
the supernatural sanction of hell-fire, to which
all who opposed were unhesitatingly consigned.
In the ages when the Christian Church was
still more than half pagan this was a formidable
weapon to wield against recalcitrant sovereigns.

The secular quarrel between the religious
and the civil power springs eternal out of the
single claim of ecclesiastics to obey and admin-
ister a higher law than the law of the land, a
claim by no means restricted to popes and
bishops. And a compact body governed by
such a theory of its own authority must be a
serious element in any political State, be it
Oriental or Occidental, and it ought to be no
matter for wonder that an Eastern government
should treat with some reserve the introduction into its territory of any organization em-
bodying such principles.

(5.) Although the tenets[1] of Christianity
do not fall directly within the scope of po-

[1] Some of the Chinese Emperors, however, notably K'ang-
Hsi and his persecuting son, assumed or affected a great interest
in the doctrines of Christianity.

litical consideration, yet, inasmuch as the species of morality which is inculcated among the people must be coloured to some extent by the doctrines which they are taught, and as the morality of a nation can never be a matter of indifference to any statesman,[1] it follows that even the dogmas of the Church may be by no means devoid of interest for him. To China in an especial sense would this observation apply, seeing that the paternal rule of the emperors includes the functions of Pontiff and public preceptor, which are continued downwards through every grade of the official hierarchy. From this point of view the apology attached to the toleration clauses in China's foreign treaties cannot be said to be irrevelant, however inadequate it may be.

Now, on this branch of the inquiry, the bearing of ecclesiastical dogma, the drama of Christianity will speak to the student in tones varying greatly according to the ear with which he listens to them. They will often appear discordant, and not seldom contradictory. In

[1] "The state can never be indifferent to the morals of the people." — Prof. SCHAFF.

the manifold divisions of the Christian mass he
will be apt to be bewildered at first, but certain lines of cleavage will gradually reveal
themselves. For example, he will find the
Church in successive ages unequally divided
between the ethical principles of Faith and
Works, or personal and vicarious merit. On
one side, creeds and ceremonial ; on the other,
virtue and charity appear in the ascendant; a
moral antithesis sufficiently pronounced. At
certain epochs, indeed, he may find official
Christianity practically divorced from morals
and wedded to the fiercer passions. Other
planes of cleavage would bring into view other
great opposed principles which are grounded
in human nature and have their full development in the Christian Church. The Stoic
ideal of duty, without compensation, and the
Epicurean ideal of pleasure, be it present or
posthumous, may be seen dividing between
them, though unequally, the field of Christian
ethics much as they did that of the pre-Chris-
tian time in the West, and do now that of the
philosophic schools of China.[1] As it has fallen

[1] "The Stoics much resemble the Confucianists of China, and
the Epicureans are represented philosophically by a sect of

to the lot of Christendom to ransack the
treasures of antiquity and to bring together
from every region of the earth the things
most worthy to be preserved, the student
will be able to recognize in its manifestations most of the time-worn psychological
ingredients, rearranged, like hewn stones from
ancient buildings fitted into modern edifices,
but with a distinction between the old and the
new which defies analysis ; such a difference
as that between the placid and reflective Lake
Leman and the impetuous Rhone, both formed
of the same waters.   If Christianity reproduces the old philosophies it is with a new
inspiration, for Reason, the balancing power,
has yielded to Faith, the impelling power, —
which removes mountains.   Nor is its efficacy
dependent on its formulas, since diverse forms
are seen to be equal in energy.   It is a power
which lives through errors.   It is not righteousness, though to the faithful it be counted
for righteousness.   Through good report or
bad, therefore, the secret of the world that now

Taoists, and practically by the large majority of opulent people
in China." — DR. FABER.

is, and probably of that which is immediately to follow, rests obviously with the Christians, which is a lesson well worth pondering by political students whether in the East or the West.

The direction of men's higher aspirations is indeed no trivial matter; whether the goal of life be, on the one hand, a Heaven which the refined depict as a "beatific vision," and the unrefined think of under more material images, or whether, on the other, it be duty to God and man, to be done even if the Heavens should fall.[1] Important questions, but scarce expressible in terms fit to serve practically for every day use, and at any rate outside the province of empirical statesmanship.

It is a source of chronic misunderstanding between the Church and the World that Christianity seems at no period to have appealed to political bodies by its spiritual, but by its material, or fighting qualities. Governments and peoples, as such, do not therefore come into

[1] "To be urged by the desire of heaven to the performance of virtue cannot bear comparison with doing good for its own sake." Confucian polemic. — DR. EDKINS.

direct contact with those representatives of the religion who, following the most closely in the footsteps of their great Exemplar, are the most gentle and patient, but with the trumpet blowers of the force, described in the metaphor of a Chinese Christian as the coarse rind which hides the precious fruit. It is not Edward the Confessor, but Defenders of the Faith like Henry VIII. and Philip; not Fénelon or Pascal, but Richelieu and Mazarin; not St. Francis, but Hildebrand and the Medici; not Thomas à Kempis, but Thomas à Beckett; not Augustine, but Athanasius; not Melanchthon or Erasmus, but Luther and Calvin; not George Wishart or George Herbert, but Knox and Laud; not Pedro de la Gasca and Las Casas, but Pizarro and Cortez; not Evelyn, but Cromwell; not Newman or Manning, but Walsh and Croke; or, to come nearer to our Eastern home, not Sarthou, but Anzer; not Crosset, but Griffith John that stand forth to the world as the spokesmen and sponsors for Christianity; the impersonation, in short, of the Church militant; the hard buttresses of Christianity, perhaps as necessary to its preservation as the rough shell is to the mollusc.

(6.) A deduction at once practical and obvious would be that which lies on the surface of every newspaper, that Christianity is the ruling factor in the polity of the Western nations, and exercises a controlling influence on all governments. A religious question would be seen to constitute a chronic obstacle to the assimilation of British rule in Ireland; the Church would be seen to hold the balance of power in Germany, compelling the strongest parties to reckon with it; nor in France, Italy, and Spain is there any political force of equal energy. The happy circumstances of the United States, which profit by the long experience of old Europe without being fettered by its traditions, enable that government to maintain perfect equilibrium among all divisions of Christianity, and enable the Churches to eliminate the grosser political elements from their religious life; while among no people is the religious principle properly so called more efficient as a social[1] force. Were it ever possible for one nation to copy another, there is

---

[1] "Christianity is the most powerful factor in our society."— Prof. SCHAFF.

perhaps no model which China would be safer in following than the United States in her dealing with Christian organization; but the peculiar difficulties of China, which are non-existent in the Western Republic, render the American example unavailing, except so far as it may furnish the idea of religious toleration on a sympathetic basis.

(7.) Perhaps the section of Christian history which would come home most directly to a Chinese politician — as it has in fact done — would be the evolution of the protectorate of the Christian inhabitants of non-Christian countries, against the civil government, by the forces of Christian states. The necessity for repelling Mohammedan invasion drove Christianity into forming political and military leagues; and among the lasting results of the protracted struggle for life between the two religions, the assumed right of Christian States to interpose between the Ottoman Government and its Christian subjects, an assumption extended in principle to all non-Christian countries, is one which possesses for China a very practical significance.

A Chinese who had the desire to follow up
the study of the natural history of Christianity would find a wealth of inviting material
all round him in the libraries of the West.
But he might thus become familiar with the
great landmarks without discovering the fruitful lands which lie between them — if the
metaphor may be stretched so far — for the
striking incidents of its outward career bear
much the same relation to essential Christianity
as the wars of a nation do to the common life
of the people.   And as the secrets of nature
elude scientific research, so will the vital principle of Christianity elude the scrutiny of any
objective critic.[1]   The mere political observer,

[1] "The real history is underneath all this.   The wandering
armies are, in the heart of them, only living hail, and thunder,
and fire along the ground.   But the Suffering Life, the rooted
heart of native humanity, growing up in eternal gentleness, however wasted, forgotten, or spoiled, itself neither wasting, nor
wandering, nor slaying, but unconquerable by grief or death
became the seed ground of all love, that was to be born in due
time; giving, then, to mortality, what hope, joy, or genius it
could receive; and — if there be immortality — rendering out of
the grave to the Church her fostering Saints, and to Heaven her
helpful angels.   Of this low-nestling, speechless, harmless, infinitely submissive, infinitely serviceable order of being, no Historian ever takes the smallest notice, except when it is robbed,
or slain." — RUSKIN.

however, would be short-sighted who failed to
take account of the moral achievements of
Christianity in disciplining the lower and culti-
vating the higher tendencies of humanity, for
without attempting any hypothetical recon-
struction of the world as it might have been
without Christianity, the myriad meliorating
agencies which draw their life blood from its
exhaustless stream are patent to common view.
The alleviation of distress, the raising of the
dejected, the purification of domestic life, the
humanizing of man and the ennobling of
woman appeal to all open minds, and the
chief credit of these things it would not be
easy to deny to Christianity. It would nevertheless be an error, as before said, to suppose
that a non-Christian Oriental would be impressed by them in the same way as a Christian
is, for wide as may be their divergences in
practice the theories of morals in East and
West are not so disparate but that such observed virtues of the West as approved themselves to an Oriental he would be inclined to
refer to the teachings of his own sages.

V.

CHRISTIANITY IN CHINA.

OUR supposititious inquirer would naturally be prompted as he went along to apply the results of his observations of the West to the circumstances of the Christian movement in China. Nor could any exercise be more practical. For China is by no means inexperienced in Western religions, and is not altogether dependent on the knowledge of them derived from abroad. She has indeed the unique advantage of being able to judge them by the comparative method, for besides having found accommodation for the two incongruous foreign systems, Buddhism and Mohammedanism, she is still struggling with the recrudescence of Christianity, which had originally gained access to the empire by the Western frontiers in the seventh century, during the T'ang dynasty. It is a fact which should interest students of comparative religion, as well as propagandists,

that the Nestorian Christianity introduced at
that early period into China, and received with
favour, was, according to the Chinese view, gradually superseded by Mohammedanism, even
as the corrupt Churches in the West had been,
but apparently without violence, Islam holding
its ground to the present day. The Christian
missions in Asia would be an attractive study,
were it only for the heroism with which their
record is enriched. Two features common to
all these efforts — whether in India, Persia,
Tibet, among the Khanates of Central Asia, or
in China — seem deserving of special note.
First, that the Christian missionaries were
nearly always welcomed and protected by the
rulers of the various states, by those even who
were already devoted to other religions. And
secondly, the missions, prosperous at the outset,
experienced violent reactions, as if their after-
taste was found bitter. It would be easy to
give local and partial explanations of this universal experience; as the awakened jealousy
of the Lamas in Tibet, the reversal of the con-
ciliatory attitude of the first missionaries towards native customs and philosophies in

China, dynastic revolutions, and so forth. But such particular reasons seem scarcely adequate to explain the entire disappearance of mediæval Christianity and the subsequent partition of Asia between Buddhism and Mohammedanism. In China the Church fared best, for there the Nestorians were still vigorous enough, after six centuries, to be a thorn in the side of the Catholic missionaries who came to, and were well received at, the Mongol Court in the reign of that model of religious toleration, Kublai, who honoured equally the four prophets, Jesus Christ, Mohammed, Moses, and Buddha.[1] From the accession of the Ming dynasty, however, communication with the West being cut off, the traces of Christianity were so completely lost that there were none either to welcome or oppose the apostles who 250 years later made their way to China round the Cape of Storms, and discovered that it was Cathay.

[1] "In this empire there are men of all nations under the sun and monks of all sects; and as every one is permitted to live in whatever belief he pleases, the opinion or rather the error, being upheld that each one may effect his salvation in his own religion, we are enabled to preach in perfect liberty and security." *Letter of André de Pérouse from Kai Tong, 1326.* — HUC.

The entrance of the Italian missionaries into
the empire and the capital towards the end of
the 16th century is described by the Chinese
— and it is their version we are concerned
with — as crafty and insidious. The missionaries, indeed, gave much the same account of
themselves, for they, by the most admirable
perseverance under almost insuperable difficulties, contrived to enter the service of the Emperors while remaining strictly under the orders
of the Propaganda. They were from the first
opposed by Censors and high officers, but were
supported by the reigning Emperor of the
Ming dynasty (Wan Li, 1573), their passport
to the imperial favour being their astronomical
science, which enabled them to correct the calendar, a task on which Hindu Buddhists had
been similarly employed seven centuries before,
and which seems still to have continued to
baffle the Astronomical Board of Peking.
Matteo Ricci, the first who gained entrance to
the Capital, had already been some years in
the Southern provinces, and there were already
more or less prosperous missions at Nanking
and several other places, described by the

missionaries as "four light-houses" diffusing
the truth over the Chinese empire. Though
constantly denounced by Ministers and Censors they maintained their ground in the provinces until the Emperor, at last yielding to
the official pressure, issued an order for them
to withdraw, which the missionaries were very
dilatory in obeying, and for a time they suffered
grievously in the provinces. In the meanwhile the religion had been spreading rapidly
throughout the empire, and counted among
its adherents men of rank and learning.
Adam Schaal, who had succeeded Matteo Ricci
in Peking as mathematician in the last years
of the Ming, and was impressed into taking
part in the military operations which ended in
its overthrow, was prompt to pay his court to
the Emperor Shun-Chih, the first of the Ta
Ts'ing dynasty, and he and his comrade Verbiest were by that monarch appointed President and Vice-president of the Astronomical
Board.

The position of these missionaries and their
followers was incessantly attacked by Chinese
officials, but during the long reign of K'ang

Hsi (1662–1723) they were still upheld by the
Emperor, who highly valued their scientific
services. But the opening of churches in the
provinces had been definitely forbidden about
1670, though the missionaries in the imperial
service were still allowed to hold religious
worship in the capital, but for themselves alone,
the propaganda being interdicted. Both re-
strictions were, however, evaded, the imperial
edicts fell into desuetude, and the propaganda
continued active in the Southern provinces.
The official pressure on the Emperor was
strenuously renewed, and in the 56th year of
his reign (1717) he was at last prevailed on to
revive the lapsed edict of 1670 and decree
the expulsion of all the foreigners, within six
months, due precautions being taken, however,
to protect them on their long journeys from
the districts in which they had settled to the
port of embarkation. Six years later the expulsion had still not been effected, and the Viceroy of Canton, Kung, then memorialized the
successor of K'ang Hsi near the beginning of
1725 to the effect that the numbers of the
foreigners were too great to be disposed of in

such a summary fashion, for the wharf at Macao
was too narrow and the available ships too few !
He therefore petitioned that they should have
leave to reside in Canton in their own establishment, but not to teach their doctrines;
and that the Chinese who had joined that sect
should be made to abandon it. The year after,
the same viceroy memorialized the Throne that
foreigners had been resident in Macao for 200
years, that their numbers had increased to
over 3,000, and he prayed His Majesty Yung-
chêng to issue an edict limiting the numbers
and ordering that the supernumeraries should
be made to leave the country, — to which the
Emperor assented.

Nevertheless, during the reign of K'ien-
Lung (1736–1796) the missionaries continued
their proselytizing efforts in the northern and
western provinces, though from the central
provinces of Hunan, Hupei, and Kiangsi they
had been hunted out and expelled. The Emperor was constrained to issue a forcible edict
ordering the searching out and prohibiting of
the sect, but always, like his predecessors, inclined to clemency, K'ien Lung in the fiftieth

year of his *reign* (1785) issued another edict
formally and in set terms confirming the pre-
vious one, which had again been secretly violated by the " preaching criminals, whose only
purpose was to propagate their doctrines, and
in no other way did they offend against the
law." Yet as they were ignorant of the law
of the empire he had pity on their sufferings
in prison, and would set them at liberty and
allow them to live in their own establishment
in the capital.

Attempts were made in 1794 by Lord Ma-
cartney, who was well received by K'ien Lung,
and again in 1816 by Lord Amherst, who was
not received by Kia K'ing because he refused
the *k'ou-t'ou* which he pretended was due to
the " Lord of Heaven " alone, to obtain more
favourable consideration for foreigners. " From
that time," says the narrative we have been
following, " began the dissatisfaction."

The Christians continued to violate the law,
evangelists went out secretly into every province, and evil people under cover of their name
accomplished their evil purposes. The risings
during the Ming, and in the reigns of K'ien-

Lung, and Kia-K'ing of the present dynasty are set down to the White Lily and other corrupt sects, which are generally associated in the public mind with the Christians.

Then, to crown all, the English forced themselves into China, bringing their "Jesus books," scattering them among the people, who have ever since been carrying on their wickedness under this cover. The English treaty of Nanking in 1842 was followed by a French treaty in 1844, which conceded protection to missionaries and other foreigners at the open ports, but did not annul the prohibition against foreigners teaching in the interior; and when the French came a second time in 1846 to Canton and urged the removal of the proscription, the Emperor Tao-Kwang decreed that at the ports they might erect Churches and the natives might there receive instruction, "but they were not to beguile women into vile practices nor by deceit take out the eyes of sick persons."

After another war the treaties extorted from China in 1858–60 granted a more general protection to evangelists and their converts in the interior of the country, and provided moreover for the restitution to the French Minister of all the buildings and lands, the property of the missions, which had been confiscated during the persecutions. After these treaties, the Chinese followers of the missionaries, trusting in the foreigners for protection, insulted the soldiers and people, and disregarded the officials, which provoked a decree from the Emperor, in which he says : " It appears from the statement in the French treaty that the sect exhort men to righteousness; this has already been published abroad. Now, recently in every province the followers of this sect and their opponents are constantly quarrelling and fighting. Hereafter let the local magistrates in every province diligently examine into the origin of these troubles and use authority to preserve the peace. If the Christians can quiet their own, let them as a body be fully protected. But if any, relying upon his sect, does evil and violates the law, then the magistrates shall certainly, according to law, try and punish his crime."

This cursory view of the advent of Christianity into China is taken from a recent collec-

tion of carefully edited Chinese State papers
called King-sz-wen, sometimes known as the
" Blue Books " a section of which, translated
by Rev. D. L. Anderson, appears in the *Chinese Recorder*, 1891. It presents the foreign
religion as seen with Chinese eyes, and considering the hostile feeling of the editor, the language of this historical section is singularly
moderate in tone, though other parts of the
compilation contain grossly offensive matter.
As a narrative of the progress of Christian
missions it is bald, and defective even in historical symmetry. The famous quarrels between
the different orders of missionaries, which on
their own showing were more ruinous to their
cause than the hostility of the Chinese, their
reference of their disputes on abstruse theological questions to the Emperor, and their appeals to Rome on matters concerning Chinese
customs and doctrines, which are made much
of by foreign critics, are passed over in silence
by this official Chinese editor, although they
would apparently have furnished material useful for his argument. And as a matter of
course the heroism of the Chinese as well as

foreign martyrs to the faith, the reports of
which drew from Pius VII. the exclamation:
" It is like a passage from the annals of the
primitive Church ! " is entirely ignored in
these publications. Necessarily, also, the hidden source of the Christians' fortitude and the
motive energy of their action were blank mysteries to those whose sympathies were with the
persecutors, and not with their victims. Neither have the devoted and disinterested lives
of the early missionaries such as Ricci and
Verbiest, which have drawn tributes of the
warmest admiration from candid Protestant
writers, made any noticeable impression on the
Chinese official world. That side of the question, however, has received such full attention
from the missionary writers themselves, almost
to the entire exclusion of the Chinese official
and popular view of their case, that it would be
superfluous to reproduce here any portions of
their vivid descriptions. It is the pure Chinese view of the mission question, with all its
defects and partialities, with which we are now
particularly concerned.

The opposition to the entrance of Christianity is, by the above narrative, shown to have been unwavering on the part of responsible officials, who laboriously reasoned against it as they also have never ceased to do against Buddhism, on general as well as on doctrinal grounds. To such attacks the missionaries laid themselves open, more, perhaps, than was absolutely necessary, for as if the Christian dogmas proper did not present a large enough mark for assailants, they cumbered their ship, as the Buddhists had done theirs, with a deck-load of perishable cosmogony, from which the Church has never been able quite to disentangle itself. The scholars and officials dwelt forcibly also on the political danger of Christianity. But a succession of emperors of gentle disposition who, suspecting no evil, treated them in a hospitable manner, allowed the missionaries to gain a footing in the Palace under the cover of teaching science, while all the time "these foreigners had their minds fixed on other unlawful things." And referring to the reparation insisted on by France in 1858 for the death of Father Chapdelaine, the reporter says: "From that time the disciples of

the missionaries, though Chinese, have become very bold, openly relying upon the
foreign Consuls to protect them, at the same
time looking with contempt upon their own
officials." [1]   He also attributes various risings in the country in former times to the influence of divers sects, and says: " All these
troubles came about through the instrumen-
tality of unemployed evil men among our
people. These made use of those worship-
ping assemblies to collect money, and a
crowd having gathered, they plotted rebellion.
. . . So from the days of Kai-K'ing to the
present, seditious plottings have been carried
out in every province. . . . Thus in all the
provinces there was no seditious sect that
did not pretend themselves to be a worship-
ping body."

These prohibitions of the teaching of Chris-

---

[1] " The native priests are said to be quite overbearing in
claiming access to the mandarins. Nor has this been entirely
confined to the Roman Catholics, but native preachers connected with Protestant Missions are also charged with demand-
ing admission into the presence of the local officials and
presuming on their connection with foreigners to claim civil privileges." — Rev. R. H. GRAVES, *Recorder*, 1884. See also Rev.
J. ROSS, in *Recorder*, August, 1892.

tianity, were extorted from the Emperors, evidently against their better feeling, and, if one or two short and sharp persecutions prompted by personal pique be excepted, required nearly 100 years to get promulgated and 60 years more to be put in full force, so deliberate are the movements of the Chinese governing machine.   They were partially rescinded by the Treaties of 1842–4, and finally by those of 1858, both of which were imposed on China by force of arms.   But a military conqueror has no power over opinion, and it is certain that the spirit which dictated the continuous remonstrances of the high officials of the empire for two hundred years was in no way changed because a Minister, trembling for his head, signed the parchment placed before him by the plenipotentiary of a victorious invader. Neither was the feeling against Christianity likely to be soothed because the propaganda, against which they had waged unceasing war, was forced thus suddenly upon the Chinese.   These circumstances render it dangerous for foreign powers to permit the slightest relaxation of treaty observance on the part of the Chinese.

But it would be unwise at the same time not
to take account of the actual predicament in
which their treaty obligations have placed that
people.

VI.

THE SOURCES OF CHINESE OPPOSITION.

IT were much to the purpose to extract, if possible, from the record of the various Chinese persecutions the special features in Christianity which render it so obnoxious to the Chinese, but such an inquiry is somewhat hindered by the reticence of both sides. The missionaries' reports have been edited as yet only in fragments, and their case has to be largely inferred from the course of events. And as to the Chinese, it is never safe to accept too literally their statements because of their constitutional habit of avoiding on all questions a direct issue, and of economizing truth by putting forward frivolous and irrelevant arguments rather than meet a case squarely on its merits. The construction of the Chinese mental apparatus, or the result of their social education, seems to bar the direct ingress and egress of thought, which consequently has to be filtered through a labyrinth of convolutions which arrest the solid particles and allow only the more volatile a free passage. The real conviction of a Chinese is scarcely to be fathomed by his own brother, from whom something is always held back, and is to be ascertained by acts and inferences rather than by direct affirmation, even on solemn occasions. The *obiter dicta* of Chinese statesmen would, if they could be gathered up and compared, be a safer key to the secrets of their mind than the more conscious mintage of their brain. Unless this canon of interpretation be applied to Chinese public documents, serious errors will be unavoidable.

From the favour with which, notwithstanding fierce academical and religious opposition sustained through many centuries, Buddhism was received by the government, the hospitality accorded to the Nestorians and other Western sects, and the tolerance subsequently extended to the Mohammedans, it may be inferred that the particular species of antagonism which has been evoked by modern Christianity was not felt towards those earlier

religious importations. Buddhism no doubt
captivated the popular mind in China and
Japan by supplying the great void left by the
teachings of the sages — the promise of a future
life, and a scheme of retribution; paradise, and
remission of sins. The entrance of Mohammedanism may have been made easy by the
purity of its deism and simplicity of ritual
offering few points of attack. Nevertheless
these two religions were not less subversive of
the indigenous theocracy of China and her
traditional superstitions than is Christianity
itself, and their comparative immunity from
persecution therefore goes towards establishing
the fact that neither a new religion, as such,
nor its foreign origin, would be sufficient of
itself to arouse the antagonism with which, in
modern times, Christian doctrine has been met
in China. The question is thus narrowed
down to such special characteristics or external
circumstances as may differentiate Christianity
from those other religious systems, and perhaps
modern Christianity from its older forms.

In the memorials of censors and statesmen
in the reigns of K'ang-Hsi and of Wan Li of

self, but also called hither fellows of his own
sort to assist in corrupting our people?" But
his chief argument was based on the disasters
which Christianity was sure to bring upon the
State: "After a while, when trouble comes,
will these converts contend against their fathers
and brothers, or will they help them? . . .
According to my humble judgment it is
better that we should be without a good
calendar than that we should have foreigners among us. . . . I fear that if we have
foreigners among us they will, by scattering their gold, gather up the hearts of the
people of our empire like as if one should carry
fire into a pile of straw fuel, and misfortune
will come speedily." In a word, the effect of
the doctrine, according to Yang, was to sub-
vert the relation of father and son, prince and
people, or, as certain earlier conservatives in
another part of the world expressed it, to "turn
the world upside down." Conscious that his
attacks would be set down to interested motives,
he declared he would gladly be misconstrued
by his contemporaries if only he could escape
being honoured by posterity as a true prophet

of China's distress. From the prominence given to his anti-Christian writings after a lapse of 200 years, it would appear that posterity really gives Yang the credit which he professed himself so anxious to avoid.

The course of the anti-Christian agitation in China has been a consistent and unbroken one, gathering strength as the religion, or its professors, became better known, and reaching its culmination in our own day — though repressed in overt action — under the double stimulus of the spread of the sects, and of the foreign treaties which protect them. From first to last, with perhaps one exception, the Emperors have been more liberal or less apprehensive of danger than their Ministers, and seemed always well pleased to command the skilled service of the missionaries on easy terms. The opposition, although fed from divers sources, such as personal jealousy, philosophical antipathy and religious sentiment, seems to have centred itself on two principal points: the dread of the political usurpation and the popular aversion. For it was natural that the people should feel at least a preliminary repugnance to a sect which contravened old customs, which kept aloof from local celebrations, which held quasi-secret meetings, and aroused distrust by the alleged practice of arts incomprehensible to the common people, and associated with witchcraft even by the educated classes.

The opposition of religionists as such, *e.g.*, the Buddhist or Taoist sects, seems never to have been very formidable; and the implied subversion of the root religion of the State — the worship of the True God by the Emperor — failed even to arouse the anger of the emperors themselves, the parties it might be supposed most directly concerned in the maintenance of the theocratic status.

Williams quotes, and paraphrases, the principal causes of trouble between the converts and their countrymen, as recorded by Monseigneur Saint-Martin, who was Vicar-Apostolic of Sechuan from 1772 to 1784 : —

FIRST. Christians are frequently confounded with the members of the Triad Society, or of the White Lily sect, both by their enemies

and by persons belonging to those associations.

SECOND.   The Christians refuse to contribute to the erection or repair of temples, etc.

THIRD.   Betrothals are almost indissoluble
in China; and whenever the Christians refuse
to ratify them by proceeding to a marriage
already commenced, they are regarded as law-
breakers and treated as such.

FOURTH.   All communications with Europeans being interdicted, the magistrates seek
diligently for every evidence of their existence
in the country, by searching for the objects
used in worship, as crosses, breviaries, etc.

FIFTH.   The little respect the converts have
for their ancestors.

SIXTH.   The Converts are obliged to take
down the ancestral tablets in order to put up
those of their own religion, and they are seldom
forgiven for this.

SEVENTH.   The indiscreet zeal of neophytes
in breaking the idols or insulting the objects
of public worship, is one of the commonest
causes of persecution.

towards corroborating the *bona fides* of both. Beliefs and sentiments, however irrational, which thus well up spontaneously at such distant periods of time and among peoples so unknown to each other, are evidently too firmly planted in human nature to be eradicated either by argument or rougher measures. To the present day there are communities in Europe who believe in abominations being practised by Jews on Christian children, and the cruelties to which that persecuted race have been subjected in every country where they have settled constitute a standing proof of the endurance of racial and religious prejudice. Gradually, under the solvent influences of time and enlightenment, such notions will doubtless die the slow death of superstitions, but the strong hand indiscreetly applied to them is apt to harden prejudices which will yield only to invincible forbearance.[1]

[1] Of course the true root of the aversion lies deeper than all that. Dr. Faber points at it (*Messenger*, July, 1892): "The Chinese have learned from the Roman Catholics and from their hundred years of struggle against Christianity to fully realize that the propagation of this religion concerns nothing short of the *very existence of the Chinese peculiar theory of life in its en-*

The practical statesman, on either side, will therefore most profitably concentrate his attention on the one point of the assumption of political power — whether intended or not intended — by the teachers and converts to Christianity, which is the most obvious source of anxiety to the Chinese government.[1]

There is not, of course, an individual missionary, nor any one of the sects into which the force is divided, who would not warmly repudiate any design of interference with the internal administration, and in most cases with the purest sincerity. But protestations have, unfortunately, no influence whatever on the course of events, for it is not by the malice prepense of individuals that dangers to the State are set up, but by the natural evolution of

tirety." Perhaps the word "theory" even puts too formal a limitation on the Chinese feeling, for something more vital and more diffusive than a mere "theory of life" seems required to account for such infinite variety and intensity of expression, and to prompt such spontaneous action, where the propagation of Christianity is concerned.

[1] "As far as religion is concerned the Chinese are not only reasonable, but extremely tolerant, till the professed religion assume, or is believed to assume, a political aspect." — Rev. J. Ross, *Chinese Recorder*, August, 1892.

their principles. Not that in this connection individuals are always free from blame, for many could be named who really have arrogated authority, given themselves official rank, or who have at least exacted the deference and assumed the state belonging to such rank,[1] who have in some cases even levied military forces, — to be used in aid of law and order, be it admitted, — and some who have dabbled in palace intrigues of a worldly character. And although hundreds more could be pointed out who bear themselves with perfect humility among their neighbours, their influence, within the purview of state government, is almost unappreciable. It has been a long standing

[1] The often quoted observation of Father Ripa, quoted because of its obvious candour, is to the following effect :

" If our European missionaries in China would conduct themselves with less ostentation and accommodate their manners to persons of all ranks and conditions, the number of converts would be immensely increased, for the Chinese possess excellent natural abilities, and are both prudent and docile. But they have adopted the lofty and pompous mannei known in China by the appellation of ' Ti-mien.' Their garments are made of the richest materials ; they go nowhere on foot, but always in sedans, on horseback, or in boats, and with numerous attendants following them. With a few honourable exceptions, all the missionaries live in this manner."

grievance of the government that the foreign priest trains his flock to look to him for protection instead of to the constituted authorities.

The simple fact of any considerable number of the inhabitants separating themselves from the general population must be a source of uneasiness to rulers, and the whole stream of official records proves that the secret sects are the chronic bugbear of the government of China. Christianity is not only reckoned as one of the sects, but it is the most difficult to manage because the autonomy to which it tacitly aspires is always, in these days, liable to be backed by foreign force. Hence the terror with which some, and the aversion with which others, of the local officials regard communities of Christians.

In Protestant journals the question is sometimes discussed whether, and how far, it is judicious for the foreign missionaries to plead the cause of their converts before local magistrates in cases where the secular interests of the Christians are involved ; and it is assumed that the native converts sometimes abuse the advantage they derive from the support of their foreign pastors with "the Consul" behind them, to claim privileges which on their merits as mere Chinese they would not dare to do.[1] Whatever conclusion may be eventually arrived at in these literary discussions, the fact of the subject being so treated at all goes far to justify the whole contention of the Government. In many parts of the country clan fights are provoked by the Christians presuming on their missionary protection. The very latest persecution, that in Pakow, in Mongo-

[1] "A missionary receives a report from one of his Church members that his heathen neighbour is persecuting him. He applies to the mandarin, who refuses to see him. Then he goes to his Consul. His Consul reluctantly refers it to the higher Chinese authorities. They send down a *wên shu* ordering the local mandarin to stop persecution. The native convert has never appealed on his own account to the mandarin. On examination it may or may not turn out a bogus concern altogether. Ten to one it is an insignificant affair. . . . But the remoter consequences are not insignificant. The Christian has been taught to lean upon a protection he is not entitled to ; the heathen feels that he is being tyrannised over by the hated foreigner, who, according to his notions, has no business to be in the country. The mandarin has been snubbed for no fault of his own; the higher officials feel that in admitting the missionary they pulled down a house over their heads, and the Consul wishes the missionary and his peddling concerns far enough." — Rev. G. T. CANDLIN, in *Manchester Guardian*, 21st December, 1891.

lia, in November last, was but the eruption of
one of those smouldering feuds. The Christians there being numerous and compact had incurred the enmity of their heathen neighbours,
particularly of the *Tsai-li*, or Abstinence Sect,
to whom, it is said, they gave much provocation. In law suits, the magistrate, intimidated
by the presence of the foreign priest, and apprehensive of censure from Peking if he should
furnish any pretext to the foreigner to appeal
to his Minister, favoured the Christian liti-
gants so openly as to excite mutiny in the
neighbourhood, which resulted in a massacre
of the Christians. If the records of the empire were fully searched, such cases, though
not all so grave, would probably be found
common enough to account for a general resentment against a perennial source of trouble
and personal risk to the officials throughout
the country.

Such military exploits as those of Monseigneur Fauré in Kueichow, and Monseigneur
Delaplace in Chekiang, although serving the
cause of the government in a crisis that threat-
ened danger to its existence, could not but open

the eyes of Chinese statesmen to possibil-
ities of a different kind. These two prelates
were loyal men, of whom one died in Kwei-fu
in 1871, and the other lived to enjoy the confidence of the Chinese government as Vicar-
Apostolic in Peking. But who would stand
sponsor for their successors, who in some similar emergency might wield similar power, but
employ it to a different end? Indeed, certain
defiant expressions of Monseigneur Deflesche
in Sechuan, during the troubles there about
1870, intimated to the French Government
that the Church in that province had confidence in its own means of self-protection. A
nation would hardly be in a satisfactory position which was liable to have to treat with an
alien in its midst at the head of troops of his
own raising, whether in the capacity — so easily
interchangeable — of ally or enemy. Her experience of her Mohammedan subjects would
alone render China suspicious and irritable in
face of separate communities in either guise.
For though in that religion itself there is
nothing inimical to the government any more
than there is in Christianity, yet the circum-

stance of a numerous body of co-religionists
thrown together by their alienation from the
people round them is a skeleton always in the
cupboard. The nucleated body must ever be
harder than the mass in which it is imbedded,
as was illustrated with costly vividness in the
two great Mohammedan rebellions in Yüman
and in Kashgar, which arose and were quelled
within the present generation, after sacrifices
which taxed the resources of the empire to the
uttermost.

Her standing warfare with the sects and
secret societies, therefore; the many insurrec-
tions these have raised in the past; the devas-
tations of Taipings, Panthays, and Dunganis,
and the waste of life and property incidental to
their overthrow; would seem to justify the
fears of China in regard to the advance of any
foreign religion; and of all the sects and societies which have yet appeared Christianity is
certainly not the one that has in general
proved to be the most docile. If, indeed, the
government officials were willing, or were in a
position, to observe the gentler fruits of Christian teaching, their political apprehensions

might be somewhat allayed; for they would see in many rural villages throughout the country the leaven of the new faith working its way in the silent manner in which the eternal forces always do work ; and they would see, if they had eyes for such things, evidences of amelioration in the life of the people, cleanliness and kindliness spreading, intelligence awakened, the desire for knowledge implanted, reading taking the place of gambling in the cottages, and the conditions of existence sweetened, brightened, and elevated for many a poor family. Equally in Catholic and Protestant mission stations might such peaceful progress be witnessed, not as the result of either Catholic or Protestant polemics, or of exciting literature, but of the personal magnetism of men and women whose lives reflect the light of love. Unfortunately, however, but inevitably, the features of Christianity which challenge the attention of the outer world, and especially of rulers, do not belong to that class, but to those which are associated with aggressiveness. It is for such phases of the religion alone that state regulations are required, just as the ordinary laws of a country have the appearance of ignoring its orderly citizens and are ostensibly concerned only with the minority who violate the social order.

Nor is it reasonable to expect the Chinese government to be more Christian than the Christians themselves; and whatever may be the intrinsic merits of the religion as expressed in the lives of saints and the death of martyrs, the most eloquent apology could not speak to a heathen government in such cogent language as the acts of the representatives of Christian governments with whom it has daily intercourse. The Chinese may be lacking in spiritual perception, but they cannot be denied the quality of common shrewdness, which enables them to take a fairly correct gauge of the foreigners of all classes with whom they come in contact, and of their motives of action. What, then, are they to think of the sacredness of a religion of which they see foreign powers competing for the championship merely in order that they may make political capital out of it to vex China; or, baser still, in order that they may make common merchandise of the Christian Church?

It seems superfluous again to repeat, that
China has not alone, indeed scarcely at all, to
weigh the inner character of Christianity ; but
to contemplate the Church in alliance with
powerful nations who, whether treating religious
affairs as ancillary to their own ambitions, or
being goaded by the Church to action against
their will, in either case make her cause their
own.   China has had memorable experience of
such, to her, ill-omened alliances.   It was the
death of a Catholic priest, whose residence in
the interior at the time was illegal, that furnished Napoleon III. the pretext for invading
China and sacking the Palace.   It was alleged
persecutions in Cochin-China that furnished,
at the same convenient juncture, the pretext to
France to take possession of that territory, and
was the not very remote cause of the Tong-
king war which lately cost China 60 million
taels, besides the loss of the protectorate.   Thus
the blood of the martyrs has been the seed of
foreign colonial empire, of whose aggrandize-
ment China has had to pay the cost.

The experience of China, so far as it has yet
gone, therefore, is not out of keeping with the

record of Christianity elsewhere. And traits now exhibited in China, which are found to correspond with those observed in remote times and places, may not unfairly be taken as practically inseparable from the only forms of Christianity which have been able to assert themselves amid the strife of nations, however much these characters may seem at variance with the principles enunciated by its Founder.

VII.

THE TAIPING REBELLION.

BEYOND these general and more or less cal-
culable risks connected with Christianity, China
has had a special and perhaps unique experience of an incalculable danger of the most serious character, which calls for some notice here.
The Taiping rebellion, which wasted the richest
provinces of the empire during a space of
fifteen years (reducing populous cities to rub-
bish heaps and fertile lands to deserts), and
which has been estimated by some to have reduced the population one way and another by
50 million souls, or according to Dr. Wells
Williams, 20 millions, was the direct outcome
of Christian teaching. Dr. Edkins calls it
" the Christian insurrection." Few nations
have had to endure the like, and a State that
has recently passed through such a life-and-
death struggle may be pardoned a little cool-

ness towards the propagation of the doctrines
with which the movement was associated.

The Protestant missionaries then in China
were elated at the outburst of the great Rebellion, not because they cherished enmity to the
government which apparently was about to be
overthrown, but because of the demonstrated
success of their teaching. It was not their
fault that the country was being desolated;
that was one of the incidents of warfare, and
the imperialists were at least as ruthless as the
rebels; but certain sacred names were blazoned
in the Rebel proclamations, and in their books
and tracts. Such is fanaticism. Let Heaven
and Earth perish,[1] so that our scheme of verbal theology may triumph. For eight years,
and perhaps longer, the Protestant missionaries
continued to be partisans of the Rebels,[2] and
one of the most experienced of them, at the

---

[1] "Among Christians there is, we are sorry to say, too large a
party that would rather allow heaven and earth to go to pieces
than confess a mistake on their part."— Dr. FABER.

[2] They had also the contemporary (1856) sympathy of the
too-soon forgotten Thomas Taylor Meadows, whose valuable
work on China stands on the shelves of a certain circulating
library these many years, uncut.

head-quarters of the chief, was enthusiastic over the orthodoxy of the junior leaders whom he personally cross-examined in the presence of, among others, the present writer, as late as 1861. The tide eventually turned, and in view of the decidedly polygamous proclivities of the Wang himself, and some rather serious aberrations in doctrine, the missions [1] gradually withdrew their sympathy, washed their hands of the new Christians — Dr. Williams calls them " these misguided men " — and passed by on the other side.

This was very well for the foreign evangelists, but what of the Chinese government? It could not blow hot and cold, but had to make up its mind and meet the calamity, whether in its quasi-orthodox character, as it appeared when viewed from a distance, or in its more heretical aspect when seen at closer quarters. And what of the fifty, twenty, or were it even but ten, millions of victims? Their ghosts assuredly would be little solaced by the news that after all certain flaws had been found in

[1] The Catholic missions were adverse to the rebellion consistently from first to last.

the orthodoxy of the Rebels. It was obviously the same thing to people and government whether these scourges of theirs were sound on the *Filioque*, or not.

In his work on " Religion in China," third edition, 1884, Dr. Edkins gives an interesting though brief account of the genesis of the Taiping rebellion, which, republished thirty years after the final suppression of the rising, may be taken as the verdict by which the Protestant missionaries are, on the whole, willing to abide. " The insurrection," he says, " began in strong religious impressions derived from reading the Scriptures and tracts published by Protestant Missionaries. . . . . We see in this movement the effect of the distribution of Bibles and Christian tracts. . . . . They felt the power of Christian truth . . . but they were without guidance in comprehending the use of the Old Testament in Christian times." In plainer language the Wang drew his inspiration from the Hexateuch, and other parts of Scripture, and with his Oriental aptitude for visions, convinced himself that he was divinely commissioned to

slay his idolatrous countrymen, and to combine in his own person the missions of Joshua
and King David.[1]   The Bible, without note
or comment, working on a half-educated,
brooding, and unprepared mind!

"The Christian insurgents in China never
had the confidence of any part of the nation,"
says Dr. Edkins.   The missionaries have
nevertheless been much encouraged by the
Taipings, whose conversion they deemed an
earnest of the evangelization of China; while
the political aims and deplorable excesses of the
rebels were attributed to, if not excused by, the
absence of personal instruction by foreign missionaries, a wholly insufficient account of the
matter.

To the Chinese government and people,
however, there was no extenuating circumstance in the movement, which they always
speak of with unmitigated horror.   The imperial rescript on the report of the death of the

[1] " Supposing Clovis had in any degree 'searched the scriptures' as presented to the Western world by St. Jerome, he was
likely, as a soldier-king, to have thought more of the mission of
Joshua and Jehu than of the patience of Christ, whose sufferings
he thought rather of avenging than imitating." — RUSKIN.

Chief said with a pathos rarely found in State
papers : "Words cannot convey any idea of
the misery and desolation he caused ; the measure of his iniquity was full, and the wrath of
both gods and men was roused against him."

It is no Chimæra, therefore, that the Chinese
dread in Christianity but a proved national
peril, their vague intuitions of this having
ripened suddenly into a terrible experience.
Perhaps the gravest feature in the Taiping outbreak, considered as an episode of Christian
development, was that, although unforeseen, it
was a not unnatural result of the fermentation
of Hebrew theology and theocracy undiluted, in
minds fretting at the hardness of the problems
of life.   Regarded in the light of religious
history the great Christian insurrection was not
more extravagant in its combination of ferocity
with fervour than other moral hurricanes which
have swept over mankind, though the uncon-
scious blasphemy of its creed may perhaps put
it in a class by itself.
There is here no question as to the intrinsic
merits of the Taiping insurrection, or the true

character of its head.   Whether it would have
been better in the long run for the Chinese, or
for the human race, that the movement should
have succeeded, or whether the leader was a hero
or an impostor, are speculations which have an
interest of their own, but are out of place here,
our concern being only with the phenomena of
the rising, and with the estimate formed of it
by the Chinese government and people, who
have the pre-eminent right to judge.

The practical question is, what security have
the Chinese against a repetition of this, or some
other form of calamity?   The depths of fanaticism have not yet been sounded, nor the possible vagaries of the human heart exhausted.
Much the same evangelizing proceedings,
which incited the Taiping rebels, at least so far
as the Chinese Government can be expected to
distinguish, are being carried on without inter-
mission over a vastly wider field ; and the missionaries to-day know perhaps as little of the
ferments which they may have set up in thousands of minds,[1] as they did of the incubation

---

[1] " The Chinese — both converts and heathen — know the missionary better than the missionary knows them.   The fact . . .

of Taipingdom.   They disseminate among
unknown millions the most stimulating literature ever penned, apparently without misgivings
as to the results.

would seem to imply a strange inability on the part of the foreigner to reach that mysterious realm, the celestial mind."—
Chinese Recorder, August, 1892.

VIII.

ANTI-CHRISTIAN LITERATURE.

DR. WELLS WILLIAMS devotes a paragraph or two of that standard repository of what is known about China, *The Middle Kingdom*, to the discussion of the efficacy of propagandism by means of the printing press. "Fifty thousand books were scattered on the coast" in certain voyages of a semi-missionary character in 1836 and 1837, "and more than double that number about Canton, Macao and their vicinity." "No one supposed that the desire to receive books was an index of the ability of the people to understand them . . . if the plan offered a reasonable probability of effecting some good, it certainly could do *almost no harm.*" What kind of harm might be in the mind of the learned author is not explained, the worst fate suggested in the context for the harmless literature itself being to "be cut up for wrapping medicine and fruit, which the shopman would not do with the worst of his own books." A generation later, one mission press in Shanghai was pouring out thirty million pages annually, an amount which was more than doubled by the other mission presses; and Dr. Williams, in recording this gigantic feat,[1] adds: "The effects of this literature upon the native mind which these agencies are scattering wider every year will be apparent in the near future." No doubt; but what are the fruits already apparent? One crop ripened and garnered, as we have seen, was the Taiping rebellion. Another copious harvest is being now gathered in; the notorious Hunan publications. Vile and unmannerly though these be, they yet constitute a reply to the pressing appeal of the missionaries to the Chinese *literati*, and it is not the challenger who has the choice of weapons.[2] Of all the provinces

---

[1] "We want quality, not quantity. . . . We have an association Secretary who repeats *ad nauseam* the word millions, and whose cry is perpetually for *money*. You never hear this cry from Apostles." — Rev. R. H. COBBOLD, in *Messenger*, April, 1892.

[2] "The famous and infamous placards of the last eighteen

Hunan is the one which has been inundated with what claims to be Christian literature, and thereby Hunan has been provoked to return samples of its own. Missionaries, especially of the Protestant sects, have in generous emulation during fifty years been doing with all their might what their Founder expressly warned them not to do (Matt. vii. 6[1]), and now they stand horrified at the consequences which he foretold as precisely as if this particular case had been in his mind.

It is not, perhaps, the holy things so much as the needlessly irritating, possibly insulting, and really unedifying and unintelligible things sometimes contained in the " Christian " litera-

months are avowedly a counterblast of the Society's tracts. If the truth is to conquer the foulness of error. . . . we must be ready to stem the issuing stream by an inflow of pure literature." — Hankow Religious Tract Society's Appeal. *Chinese Recorder*, March, 1892.

1 " In pursuing the course described above [the reckless circulation of Christian literature] we have sometimes acted in direct opposition to the spirit if not the letter of our Saviour's command 'Give not that which is holy, etc.' . . . Our failing to follow the instructions of our Lord in this respect may perhaps account for the meagre and disappointing results which have followed the very extensive distribution of books for the last 40 or 50 years." — Rev. Dr. NEVIUS, *Recorder*, 1884.

ture which are the most answerable for the
filthy abuse which has been lavished on the
missionaries and their faith.   It is not of course
to be doubted that the editing[1] and circulation
of tracts and scriptures is carried out as effi-
ciently as the stupendous mass of matter dealt
with allows,[2] but until some competent and
independent sinologue assumes the task of
sifting the productions of the mission presses
the world cannot know what incentives may
have been offered unwittingly to these Chinese
revilers.   It is by no means impossible that
even the foulest of their epithets might be
traced to some unhappy expressions in original,
or translated compositions by foreign missionaries impatient to try their hand[3] before acquir-

[1] "Most of these books, as also the greater number of articles
in the newspapers put in the hands of the Christians, contain indigestible stones instead of bread." — Dr. FABER.   But what of
the *non-Christian* population of Hunan, and elsewhere?   Would
not "stones of offence" be in their case a more descriptive
term?

[2] The Hankow Tract Society issues one million tracts every
year.

[3] "Perhaps nothing has been more hurtful to missionaries in
preparing books, than haste, . . . the desire to hurry it through
the press lest some of the readers of China should die without

ing sufficient command of that double-edged weapon, the Chinese language; or of others carried away by an inflexible conviction that what is good in season and in appropriate circumstances must be good absolutely and always. Dr. Chalmers, of Hongkong, once heard a Chinese crowd laughing at the preaching of a foreigner who was incessantly repeating the Chinese name for God, *Tien-chu*. But his manner of pronouncing the words conveyed the sense of "mad pig" at every utterance of which the audience broke out into peals of laughter. *Ex uno disce omnes*. What could missionaries themselves not say on such topics would they testify? The incident is truly full of grave suggestiveness.[1]

Let it be granted that the Christian literature with which Hunan has been flooded is for the most part wholesome and void of offence. The Chinese *literati*, however, with their strong

seeing it! In a great majority of instances unprejudiced judges will be of the opinion that the world can afford to wait a little." — Rev. Dr. NEVIUS, *Recorder*, 1884.

[1] The bestial expressions complained of in the Hunan pamphlets are stated by the latest authorities to be exactly such plays on words as are indicated in the text.

prejudices and their foregone conclusion, naturally select the parts most suitable for their
controversial purposes just as the Christian
missionaries perhaps hold up the worst of the
Chinese tracts for execration. But could any
thing be more untoward than the connection
of the methods of propagandism with this ava-
lanche of bad literature which issues continu-
ously from Hunan? [1]

So far, however, are the zealous missionaries
of Hankow and Wuchang from seeing the
matter in this light that they make urgent appeals for increased means of carrying on their
duel with the Hunan pamphleteers, only claiming that their adversary be muzzled while they
redouble their efforts to silence him.

---

[1] " To oppose enmity is to increase it. . . . There is much
slang and obscene language in the streets which we, in most cases,
cannot comprehend, but may see the effects of it on the faces of
the by-standers. To go on with a religious discourse under such
circumstances would show a want of good taste and judgment on
the part of the preacher. . . . When an audience shows signs of
profanity or indifference, then, a dignified silence is the best ora-
tion. The Jews not only opposed the apostle, but they blas-
phemed. This made any further preaching among them hopeless." — DR. FABER.

With two such, and so widely different answers to their message to China before them it might seem reasonable for the propaganda to pause and consider what form the next answer may possibly take, whether in the near, or the distant future.   But it is remarkable that the missionaries, so far at least as they may be considered to be represented by the two learned gentlemen above cited, seem scarcely conscious of the possibility of evil resulting from this prodigious mass of what may be called dynamic literature.

IX.

CHRISTIANITY IN JAPAN.

SOME readers who have followed the theme thus far may possibly wonder that while frequent reference has been made to other countries there has been no allusion to the remarkable history of Christianity in Japan. But the circumstances of that country and its people are so different from those of China that it might be misleading to make any comparison, except as a matter of curiosity. Japan is a State which may be said to have always known its own mind, and acted out its opinion. When she admitted Christianity she did so heartily; when she suppressed it she did so relentlessly, but not without valid reason; and when she readmitted the religion it was as part and parcel of the general civilization of the Western nations to which by deliberate choice Japan opened wide her arms. By the promptitude of her decision Japan avoided all appearance of coercion by foreign powers. (What, by the way, does Mr. Bosworth Smith mean by his repeated references to the criminality of Great Britain's wars with Japan?) And her treaties contain no toleration clauses, nor any that are derogatory to her dignity, although an idea has been kindled in recent years that the extra-territorial stipulations do belong to that category. There is consequently no true analogy between the respective relations of China and Japan towards foreign nations, foreign religions and foreign life. The geographical proximity of the two countries does no doubt suggest to the Western world a similarity in their circumstances which, however, is only superficial; and if their opportunities of observing each other prompt some mutual emulation, that also is scarcely less superficial. Ships and guns, military drill, and material appliances may be copied, but what makes for the peace and prosperity of a nation is too deep for imitation, it must be a growth from within, nourished though it may be by atmospheric influences from without. Japan seems to be receiving Christianity in its most innocuous and enduring form, for the people are receiving it, and the pyramid is being built on the widest base. Of the many pleasing spectacles which a visit to that tourist's paradise always affords, perhaps none leaves a more agreeable impression than the decorous worship of large Japanese congregations conducted entirely by natives. And the vernacular religious press is now a recognized factor in the social system. The government there has no fears about its Christian subjects, whom it knows only as exemplary citizens; and it winks at the pious frauds of the foreign missionaries who take out passports to travel for their health or in the pursuit of science, because it recognizes that it has the propaganda well in hand. The establishment of the Catholic Hierarchy in Japan affords the most substantial proof that the government of that country has adopted a policy of benevolent toleration towards Christianity, based on the conviction that it will never have to account to foreign powers for its attitude towards either the religion or its followers. Added to which, the Japanese people are peculiarly sensitive to all foreign influences, and do not present that mass of stolid resistance which innovations encounter in China. The circumstances attending the introduction of Christianity into the respective countries, therefore, present scarcely anything but sharp contrasts, and probably no lesson for China can be drawn from Japan excepting such as could only be applied by reversing the wheel of history for fifty years, and undoing the chapter of evolution by which the new Japan itself has emerged from its secular isolation.

X.

PRACTICAL CONSIDERATIONS.

REVERTING to the proposition with which we set out, China has been compelled by nations stronger than herself to admit their religion, which, after full deliberation, she had decided to reject, and for reasons which, whether good or bad, were at least not unintelligible. Nor has any option been left to her as to which of the different forms of Christianity she would prefer; she is forced to tolerate the propagation of all indiscriminately, which is more than the nations which coerce her themselves do. In the irksome and anxious position into which they have been thrust, the leaders of the Chinese State have, so far, derived little support from either foreign statesmen or the leaders of the Propaganda. Dr. Williams himself, so long familiar to the government as *Chargé d'Affaires* for the

United States, in which capacity he must have
been largely occupied with mission affairs, had
no clearer or more practical counsel to be-
queath to China than that: "The progress
of pure Christianity" — so easy to write! —
"will be the only adequate means to save the
conflicting elements . . . from destroying
each other."

The Chinese opposition to Christianity during the last three hundred years has undoubt-
edly taken arbitrary, harsh and cruel forms,
yet considering that during nearly the whole of
that period the sovereignty of China was under
no foreign constraint, the forbearance with
which she has treated recalcitrant missionaries,
even during state persecutions, will compare
not unfavourably with the record of similar
persecutions elsewhere.

Compelled by foreign powers suddenly to
reverse the engines of state policy which had
been gathering momentum in one direction for
some centuries, the Chinese government has
met the new conditions in as accommodating
a spirit as could perhaps, under the circumstances, have been expected. At the same

time it is plain to be seen, and ought to have
been foreseen, that an act of state was not efficacious to change, as by a magician's touch, the
hearts of a nation and of a numerous official
hierarchy.

Whether the Western governments were
well or ill-advised in this exercise of their
power is now of little practical significance.
The historical transaction cannot be undone,
nor the *status quo ante* in any manner restored.
It remains only to be considered, what is
China to do with regard to this force, — in-
scrutable, indomitable, inflexible, yet, on its
own conditions, passionately benevolent?

She cannot exclude or repress it, any more
than she can exclude Influenza or the Mon-
soon. She must receive it. She has already
done so indeed, but with a bad grace — as was
natural — and grudgingly ; a most dangerous
half-measure. For she has by her treaties
given to foreign powers at least the semblance
of the legal right to call her to account if she
fails to protect Christian missionaries, while by
her furtive and wavering action she allows officials and people to furnish the foreign powers

with constant pretexts for exercising that right.
No position could be more hazardous for
China, as many of her public men, who know
something of the Western world, must be well
aware. The pressure of Christianity will never
abate; it will on the contrary augment, and if
it is difficult now to maintain an erect position
in its presence it may be impossible to do so
hereafter when the foreign religion has con-
solidated its strength. In short, unless some
other agency anticipates its slower action, Christianity may be the force destined eventually to
dissolve the Chinese, as it did the Western
empire, and to destroy the present fabric of
its society.[1]

To announce danger is easy; not so the
task of concerting measures to avert it. The
difficulty of an effective co-ordination of the
component forces of the Chinese State being
formidable, the temptation to temporize is
strong, for there is no man living, however
pessimistic, but may expect the *status quo* to
last at least his time, if not a good while beyond
it. Few there be who dare to face the unpopu-

[1] See Note p. 37.

larity which a judicious regulation of Christian
affairs would entail in a country where there is
so much to lose, so little to gain, by the active
display of public spirit.   The parallel between
the China of to-day and the Rome of 1800
years since, though imperfect and in many
respects invalid, yet in certain features runs so
close, that an imaginative Chinese might almost
read the destiny of his own country in the
events of that remote time.   The Cæsars were
tolerant of the new religion, thinking it might
mingle harmlessly with the numerous existing
systems which, like it, had come mostly from
the East.   Though in theory it violated the
laws, the Emperors were reluctant to put the
laws in force ; and though without sympathy
for the sect, they, like Kien-lung, could find
no real fault in it, and were always recom-
mending the Christians to mercy.   Nor was
the deference paid by the Cæsars to popular
sentiment very unlike that now shown by
the Chinese Emperors to provincial opinion.
Then, as now, the rulers were willing to protect Christians alike from popular violence and
official animosity, and though even Marcus

Aurelius, a man saturated with ethics, allowed himself to be constrained to issue severe edicts against the Christians, like K'ang-hsi 1500 years after him, yet as Mr. Lecky records, "the atrocious details of the persecutions in his reign were due to the ferocity of the populace and the weakness of the governors of distant provinces," a not inapt description of some of the anti-Christian outrages in modern China.

Unfortunately the experience of Rome furnishes no lessons for China except in the way of warning, and neither the ages of tumult during which the present Europe was being evolved, nor the actual position of these Western countries afford her any positive guidance; for none of them can be said to have dealt successfully with the religious problem. The United States of America, indeed, though not without a struggle, enjoy the supreme happiness of religious and political equilibrium, but that is the result of a situation absolutely unique, which cannot be imitated. The adjustment of the relations of Christianity to the Chinese State therefore can only be evolved, without direct aid from precedent, from the action of general principles which may be deduced from a diversity of experience. Religious enthusiasm is a contingent factor, on which the Taiping episode sheds but a dim light; and as to the form which Christianity will assume when eventually acclimatized in China, all that may safely be predicted is that the new amalgam will be unlike anything that has yet appeared in the world. Its main characteristics, however, will probably be to an indefinite extent determined by the circumstances of its mode of introduction. Which is a vital question for Chinese Statesmen and imperial counsellors to consider, could they but perceive its urgency.

The problem is necessarily abstruse where unknown psychological factors are concerned ; and assuredly no solution of it will be attempted here. Nor is it perhaps within the competence of any man to work out an equation containing so many unknown qualities. What may be done, however, is to indicate one or two primary canons which should govern legislative and administrative dealings with the subject, canons based on ascertained and unalterable facts. For though the end of a journey may be hidden in mist one may advance in confidence if only the first steps be in the right direction, trusting that the way may become clear as successive stages are reached.

I.   The first canon by which the relations of Christianity should be regulated may be stated without hesitation.   It is the complete fulfilment of existing obligations.   China has undertaken by treaty to protect missionaries and to tolerate Christianity, and she must protect and tolerate accordingly, without equivocation or reserve.   No matter if the obligation was imposed by force, the nation and the government stand bound to it in law, and therefore in honour, at least until they find themselves strong enough to make a fresh appeal to the tribunal under which the foreign treaties were imposed.   To protect nominally, and yet secretly persecute, or connive at persecution, is not only a device unworthy of a civilized government and of a body of highly educated men like the Chinese official class, but it is also the road to ruin.   Unless therefore the ministers who are responsible for the welfare of the State can nerve themselves to the required resolution it will be futile to discuss or manœuvre at all in this matter, for whatever they do will be vain so long as the fundamental condition of success is not complied with.

The difficulties in the way of the Chinese government so fulfilling its obligations to foreigners are partially understood, and sympathized with by foreigners. But that feeling does not diminish by a feather's weight the gravity of the duty. The Imperial government is naturally, and properly, reluctant to humiliate its Viceroys to please foreigners, who are the objects of common aversion. The Viceroys have still stronger temptations to evade their duty to foreigners whenever it requires them to reprove their own subordinates, or still worse, bring under the discipline of the law men of influence who are detached from the regular service of the State. Yet nothing less than this is imperatively required of all who occupy posts of trust in the government. It is a duty, however, which, like many others, may be harder in anticipation than in execution, and one which might evolve the needed strength by the action itself. A firm resolution on the part of the Central government to tolerate no evasions from either high or low would of itself more than half accomplish the object, and one or two conspicuous examples made of contumacious officials might achieve it altogether. When men are sincere they are usually taken at their word, and the rulers of China would find their word would pass as good current coin of the realm as soon as they gave clear proof to their servants that they intended to make it so.

Reduced to practice this canon would make short work of anti-Christian rioters and of the authors and publishers of calumnious attacks on Christians, as such. The men who have long been screened by powerful influences from the consequences of their shameless deeds would be punished like common malefactors, and the government would not wait to be stirred to action by foreign officials or public demonstrations, but would in all cases be beforehand with them, and thus leave absolutely no ground of complaint.

How far the Chinese government and ruling classes are at present from the attainment
of such a standard of national duty need not
be said.   But it cannot be too strongly re-
iterated that it is only in the full realization of
the administrative ideal thus indicated that the
government can hope to find salvation.

II. The relations between the civil authorities and the Christians should be settled and
defined.

It is too late in the day perhaps to regret
that there should ever have arisen any question
of special treatment of converts to Christianity.
It is the wisdom of China, as of other states,
to make all her people equal before the law;
and it is the foreign powers which are, prima-
rily, answerable for forcing her government to
deal with native Christians as if they really
constituted a State within the State.   But Chinese provincial officials have fallen easily into
this way of regarding them; notwithstanding
that it was opposed to the declared policy of
the empire.   (See Appendix I.)   It would indeed be hard to say which of the two parties

— the Christian or the anti-Christian — has evinced the greatest eagerness to effect the complete isolation of Christians from the body of the Chinese people. The questions deserve to be calmly weighed: — whether the segregating process shall be allowed to extend; whether it shall be arrested at the point which it has now reached; or whether even a retrograde movement towards obliteration of the legal distinction between Christian and Heathen shall be inaugurated.

The holding of property away from the commercial ports by missionaries, under the French treaties of 1858–60, seemed to necessitate the official recognition of the Mission as a corporation, since individuals could not by the rules of their Orders acquire sites or erect Churches in their own right, and so the missions naturally became identified with the congregations. But sound property legislation is one of the chief pivots on which the peace and order of communities turn; and from the Chinese political point of view it was probably a misfortune that the missions in their collective character ever obtained so

much necessary consideration from the local
authorities as to have buildings and ground
officially registered in their name.[1]

The sequel is still an unwritten chapter of
history, but hints are given from so many
quarters, native and foreign, as to leave little
doubt of the fact that congregations of Christians in the interior are prone to club together
for the common defence, and to abuse the
protection which their foreign pastors, under
the ægis of foreign treaties, are able to give
them.   It is the same spirit that prompts the
native servants of Europeans at the treaty
ports to rely on the prestige of their employ-
ers to screen them from the consequences of
their insolence to their countrymen.   Experienced missionaries have to be constantly on
their guard against plausible complaints of
injustice made to them by their converts, but
younger and more eager men, and those who
are constitutionally disposed towards partisan-
ship " rush in " where the more wary " fear to

---

[1] The Chinese government found it necessary during the
Ming dynasty, to limit the landed possessions of Buddhist mon-
asteries to 60 *mu*, or 10 acres.

tread;" and take part in village-law suits which they are able to conduct with greater ability and force than natives working on their unaided resources. It may be admitted that the habitual laxity and dilatoriness which characterize Oriental procedure offer constant temptation to impatient outsiders to intervene in order to accelerate the despatch of business. Nothing but injury to the Christian name, however, can result from such illegitimate interferences, while it is not Christianity that is really at fault, but the cupidity of men, who may have entered the Christian community solely from these secondary motives.[1]

It would seem to be a very fair thing for the Chinese government to appeal to the consideration of Western governments in this matter, and if it could but come into court with clean hands, that is to say, having scrupulously fulfilled its own obligations under treaty, the Western governments could scarcely help listening to the plaint.

[1] " Whole villages have offered to turn Christians " to gain " the powerful influences of foreigners on their side in some litigation." — Rev. R. H. GRAVES, in *Chinese Recorder*.

All foreigners residing or travelling in the
interior under passport should be strictly forbidden by their own authorities from med-
dling in any dispute between Chinese, whether
Christians or not. Such prohibition need not
in the least impair the influence of private
counsel in promoting goodwill, but as there is
no judgment in the common affairs of life
more fallible than that of the average ecclesi-
astic, of any communion, such an interdict
could not but have a salutary effect on the
peace of Chinese communities.

That some Christian pastors would vehe-
mently resist any legislation tending to disinte-
grate their Christian communities is highly
probable; and, from their point of view, they
would have valid reasons on their side. There
is doubtless this real difficulty in the way, that,
as the Chinese Christian by breaking away
from the traditions of his family and neighbours generally forfeits his status as a member
of the clan or village-community, it is natural
that he should strive to regain the lost position
through the creation of a new caste, or social

unit, — the Christian commune, with its officers corresponding to village elders, and enjoying equal legal recognition with the villages
themselves. Dr. Faber, whose logical mind
cannot rest in equivocations, claims these privileges in the clearest terms, on the broad, if
somewhat ingenious, ground, that the Christians, having by the foreign treaties been
absolved in certain matters from the law of
the land, obey the paramount Divine Law,
which gives them the right to toleration, and
toleration means privileges. It may be as
much the duty of the Christians, as such, to
prefer these claims as it is of the government
to deny them ; but there is here in fact the
germ [1] of the secular trouble between the
religious and the civil power. A Christian
body capable of unlimited expansion, following a divine law which is above the law of the
land, with the Christians themselves as its sole
interpreters, is precisely that kind of social

[1] The germ of that phase of the development of Europe
which is thus epigrammatically summed up by Ranke : " Ecclesiastical estates were no longer described as situated in certain
counties, but these counties were described as situated in the
bishoprics."

organism which any civil government may justifiably treat with reserve.[1] But how, then, it may be asked, is the adjustment between the parties to be effected, and a *modus vivendi* to be established. The government might reply that, as it is the Christians who have created the difficulty, it is for them either to find a solution or to bear the inconvenience of waiting until one is found; but that the government meanwhile has the duty to discharge of preventing any Christian or other body from getting the upper hand of the civil magistrate.

In practice, no doubt, the danger to the Chinese government from the political aspirations of Christians is much diminished by the miscellaneous character of the Christian bodies. They have divided themselves, and may be

---

[1] " To permit this would be to make the professed doctrines of religious belief superior to the law of the land, and in effect to permit every citizen to become a law unto himself. Government could exist only in name under such circumstances." — *Judgment of Chief-Justice Morrison R. Waite, in the Supreme Court of the United States.* — SCHAFF.

" If government commands us to act against conscience and right, disobedience becomes a necessity and a duty." — IBID.

more easily ruled than if they were compact;
and so a state of things which is to be deplored
from the point of view of Christian progress
serves conveniently to lighten somewhat the
burden of the government.

III.   A third canon would provide for the
preservation of peace, and the prevention of
wanton provocations between different religionists.   Rival sects should, by virtue of the
power inherent in every civilized state to maintain order among its people, be compelled to
keep their feelings under discipline in all assemblies and public places.   The objects and
the rites of Christian worship are not infre-
quently reviled or mocked, and the anger of
the worshippers thereby provoked; and, on
the other hand, it is far from uncommon for
converts, and even for missionaries themselves,
to inveigh against the native customs and the
native gods; both practices tending to breaches
of the peace, which ought therefore to be made
amenable to the law.[1]   Sometimes the attacks

[1] " If any person shall abuse or deride any other for his or
her different persuasion and practice in a matter of religion he
shall be looked upon as a disturber of the peace and be punished
accordingly." — *Laws of Pennsylvania.* — SCHAFF.

on idolatry are made in mere mockery, examples of which find their way into foreign
journals, and are presumably common in the
preaching of evangelists.[1] This is, to say the
least, bad taste; but it is more, it is an offence
against decency to cast ridicule on the honest,
however mistaken, devotions of a fellow-mor-
tal;[2] and it is an offence both against good
order and the laws of hospitality when it is
done by an alien.[3] The first Apostles of

[1] "Anybody acquainted with Chinese will soon find, if he
attends the foreign street chapels a few times, that the hostile
attitude of many missionaries towards the most cherished beliefs
and feelings of the Chinese is frequently expressed in a most
offensive manner. As for the books . . . let those interested
read some of the elementary catechisms or some of the books
dealing with ancestral worship, idolatry or other superstitions of
the Chinese, and he will find these things discoursed on in anything but a kindly spirit. Chinese hear offensive statements in
the chapels, get angry, and denounce the missionary to their
friends. They read the books . . . and determine to pay out
the hated barbarian at the first opportunity."—"A SINCERE
FRIEND TO BOTH PARTIES."—*N. C. Herald*, 26th February, 1892.

[2] "To revile with malicious and blasphemous contempt the
religion professed by almost the whole community is an abuse of
that right" [the right of "free and decent discussion."] — *Chief
Justice Kent in Supreme Court of New York, 1811.* — SCHAFF.

[3] The foreign missionaries sometimes applaud the courage
of their converts in openly reviling the false gods, and sometimes
they deplore the indiscretion of such sallies, according to circumstances and individual temperament.

Christianity were particularly tender with the religious susceptibilities of the people among whom they moved, so that the sensible magistrate, the town-clerk of Ephesus, in his address to the rioters, was able to testify that these early missionaries "were not blasphemers of our goddess." Their successors in the next two or three centuries were not so considerate; iconoclasm becoming rampant with the corruption and the triumph—almost synonymous terms—of the Church, when the great Ambrose allowed himself to scoff even at the virginity of the poor Vestals. It were a good and laudable thing if all blaspheming of each other's gods could be rigorously suppressed by the civil power. This is also a matter on which Western governments might be approached, and solicited to frame appropriate rules for the governance of their nationals. Then a foreign missionary affronting native religion in any public manner might first be warned by the local authority, and, if recalcitrant, conducted to the nearest consul for deportation, while condign punishment would be equally meted out to any Chinese who should

vituperate Christianity. Complete reciprocity
in this matter should be insisted upon, and
each party made to do as he would be done by.[1]

Two drawbacks to any such procedure will
readily suggest themselves: the laxity and
irregularity of Chinese official practice; and
the scarcely avoidable abuses by underlings.
The most difficult attainment for a Chinese
official is to maintain a just measure in the performance of his functions, — to be firm without
being harsh; and the difficulty of furnishing
foreign governments with adequate guarantees
for moderation would probably prove fatal to
any arrangement whereby new powers over
foreigners would be placed in Chinese hands.

Meagre and superficial though these sugges-
tions be, and perhaps not judiciously selected
from the heap of desiderata, they are yet so far
in advance of what is proximately realizable

---

[1] As for the sectarian quarrels of Christians *inter se*, probably no regulations could be framed to check them; but the
spectacle of two foreign missionaries meeting in a Chinese thor-
oughfare, one warning the people against the religion of Henry
VIII., and the other against the worship of a mere woman, can
hardly, one would think, advance either of the divisions of Christianity, or be approved by any reasonable man.

that it would serve no purpose of interest or utility, at this stage, to pursue that part of the subject into greater detail.

Nevertheless the procedure here recommended involves no theoretical innovation, for the principles are only those which have been explicitly and repeatedly laid down by the highest authority in the land, and are, moreover, based on the religious toleration which was worked out centuries ago, and became the settled national policy not later than the Sung dynasty, A.D. 960–1280. The Edicts of Tao Kwang may be taken as a convenient starting point for the new departure in Christian toleration (see Appendix I.), and all the State papers which have been issued during the past fifty years have been in harmony therewith. The Governor Shen Pao-chen, in 1862, developed the doctrine of toleration with a breadth of charity towards Christians which left little to be desired, and what gave the highest value to his memorials is that his expositions were not theoretical, but were suggested by specific occurrences within his official jurisdiction to which he fearlessly applied the principles deduced from his obser-

vation of facts and his knowledge of the imperial policy. The same official, when Viceroy
of Kiangnan in 1876, had occasion once more
to discuss the rules which should govern the
relations between foreign missionaries and the
Chinese people, when he pushed his former
arguments into still greater detail; his despatches convinced Dr. Edkins that Shen Pao-
chen " anticipated the spread of Christianity in
China to proceed in the same way as was the
case with Buddhism and Taoism in former
centuries." And Dr. Edkins takes Shen Pao-
chen as the mouth-piece of his government.

Tsêng Kuo-fan, than whom no more authoritative exponent of the permanent policy of
China has been known in this century, in a
memorial which was never intended for publi-
city, also lays down the same law of toleration,
for " while other religions rise and fall from age
to age the doctrines of Confucius survive un-
impaired throughout all ages." And so all
other authentic public documents.

What is needed, therefore, is to give practical effect to the declared will of the government,
and had this been done sooner, overt violence

towards the missionaries might possibly have
been avoided, however far the people might
have been from receiving their teaching.

Before, however, practically considering any
general regulations for mutual toleration, there
is one preliminary duty incumbent on the
Chinese government in order to qualify it for
entering on the discussion.   It must deal de-
cisively with obnoxious publications such as
those which are regularly issued from Hunan.
By these productions the literature of China is
stamped with indelible disgrace, for since their
offensiveness has provoked foreigners to repub-
lish them they will henceforth expose to all the
world the ignorance, vulgarity, and intellectual
prostitution of Chinese scholars, as well as their
contemptible attainments in the graphic art.
In this guise will the writers of the Ta-tsing
dynasty enjoy an immortality of infamy in all
Western lands, for these choice specimens of
their works will be preserved, like flies in amber,
in every library in Europe and America.   The
Hunan scholars will be known in future generations as those who in order to injure foreigners

did not scruple to debauch the minds of their countrymen with ideas as filthy as they are false. These disgusting books are acknowl-edged to be the efficient cause of the riots which bring humiliation on the government and penalties on the people. The names of their authors are well known, thanks chiefly to the pertinacious investigations of Dr. Griffith John, who has done admirable service in the elucidation of the history of these matters; but because they are literary graduates enjoying the protection of high personages [1] the authors have been allowed to escape the penalty of their disloyal acts. If the government be not will-ing to extinguish this source of conflagration then it is evading its obligations under the foreign treaties and making itself a participator in the crime, thus exposing itself to reprisals at the hands of foreign powers whenever it may suit their convenience to enforce their rights. If, on the other hand, the government be not

---

[1] "He (Chou Han) knows well that he is looked upon as a philanthropist, that he has the real sympathies of the officials on his side." — DR. GRIFFITH JOHN in *N. C. Daily News*, 19th April, 1892.

able to suppress this infamous literature, then it is not the Emperor who rules, but the authors and publishers of these pamphlets.   In either case these publications, so long as they are in circulation, constitute a standing inculpation of the government, which will warrant foreign powers in assuming its guilt in any given case, without further inquiry.

What is, perhaps, more serious still is that the same or similar shocking calumnies against Christians are repeated in the King-sz-wen, the collection of State papers, treaties, memorials, etc., before cited, the latest edition of which, published in 1888, came out under the auspices of Chinese officials occupying the highest position in the State.

XI.

RELATION OF CHRISTIANITY TO PEOPLE, LITE-
RATI, AND IMPERIAL GOVERNMENT.

LET it be assumed, however, that a working scheme for the treatment of Christianity based on such general principles as have been suggested shall have been elaborated and carried into effect — a very large assumption indeed — still the end of the Christian troubles would by no means have been reached. The hostility of the literary and official classes, though outwardly suppressed, would suffer no real abatement, but would smoulder, like a subterranean fire, ready to break forth whenever the repression was relaxed.

The popular suspicions also would persist virtually intact; the dread of witchcraft, the belief in secret abominations, the mutilations of the sick or dead, and all the rest, still would remain to be lived down slowly. Substituting impiety towards ancestors for atheism these imputations are substantially identical with those made against the primitive Christians in the West, where they survived through several centuries of Christian progress.   The pulses of China do not beat faster than those of the Western races, nor is the intelligence of the common people more advanced.   And if it should take a century or two for the Chinese Christians to clear their characters from these odious suspicions there is no help for it, and the Christians must even learn to bear it, until they can convert their present minority into a majority,[1] when the charges would vanish into air.   Possibly the censorious eyes of neighbours may even be a salutary discipline, keeping the converts on their good behaviour. The finer qualities of Christianity shine brightest in adversity, and the Church would be in evil case were all men to speak well of it. This reflection might even be stretched to cover persecution in general as being condu-

---

1 " We have patiently to wait till a powerful minority, if not a majority, of the Chinese people is Christianized. " — Dr. FABER.

cive to the healthy growth of Christianity ; for
to what extravagances might an unopposed
Chinese Church not run ![1] Woe, indeed, be
to him by whom the offence comes, but still,
to apply a phrase coined for a very different
occasion, to the opposition to Christianity in
China, *si elle n'existait pas il faudrait l'inventer*.

In one respect the Chinese Christians have
the advantage over their Western prototypes.
They do not themselves give countenance to
the calumnies, whereas the early Christians did
not scruple to throw at the heads of heretics
the vile accusations brought by the heathen
against themselves. Nor is it certain that such
inter-Christian amenities have entirely disappeared even yet from contemporary history in
the West.[2]

[1] " Rome is best when competing with Protestant rivals — in
the midst of hostile criticism and alien institutions ; worst when
she has it all her own way."— R. H. HUTTON.

[2] A recent occurrence in Europe illustrates the vitality of
these odious superstitions. In the town of Xanten, in Rhenish
Prussia, a boy was found in a shed dead from a wound in his
throat. Suspicion fastened at once on a Jewish butcher named
Buschoff, owing to the popular belief that the Jews require blood
at certain seasons for their religious rites, and the artistic cut in
the boy's neck being held to betray the practised hand of the
carnifex. The Christian people became so infuriated against

While waiting, however, for the populace to get their minds purged from these degrading notions something may and ought to be done by the officials and *literati* to uncover the real truth in regard to Christian practices.   They have at once the means and the intelligence to sift the facts and to prove or disprove what has been alleged.[1]   It is true that even officials and scholars are credulous enough to believe many of the slanders which are circulated about foreign missionaries.   The Emperor Tao

the Jew that, to save him from being lynched *more Americano*, the authorities took him in charge and put him on his trial.   The testimony of the witnesses was vociferous and overwhelming, the gentry corroborating the populace; but when subjected to the cool analysis of the lawyers the evidence was shown to be only crystallised gossip, the offspring of an inveterate general belief in the occult practices of the Jews.   But had not the accused conclusively established an *alibi* it might still have gone hard with him.   So great, indeed, was the excitement that the official responsible for the trial at first demanded a battalion of soldiers to keep order, the burgomaster declining to be answerable for the peace of the town.   Eventually the dignity of the legal tribunal was maintained without the resort to military force.   These things took place in the best educated country in Europe in the summer of 1892.

[1] See the emphatic contradiction of the false reports of a magistrate given in Li Hung-chang's memorial published in the *Peking Gazette* of 16–17th February.

Kwang himself, when issuing an Edict of toleration,[1] as we have seen, could not help
encouraging the belief that the Christians really
picked out the eyes of the sick. But with all
mission establishments and practices thrown
open to the inspection of Government officials
— a thing which is gradually coming to be
thought necessary — there would be no excuse
for these officials continuing in their present
state of dangerous ignorance. And when they
shall have once satisfied their own minds they
can the better clear away the doubts of the
common people by disseminating truthful reports. If the literates of Hunan are willing
to expend their time and money in printing
and publishing calumnies which befoul the
paper they are written on, it would be a small
thing for the officers of the government to
give the public the benefit of their discoveries
in the region of ascertained fact. And this
would be no more than a tardy reparation for
the injury done to the reputation of the Christians and for the debauching of the imagina-
tions of the illiterate masses.

[1] Appendix I.

Were a *modus vivendi* ever established with the populace and the *literati* the relation of Christianity to the Supreme government itself would probably present few difficulties. From the earliest appearance of foreign religions in the country the sovereign has been, as a rule, favourably disposed towards each of them in succession; and, except in the few instances where devotion to one creed biassed them against others, the Chinese Emperors have been the defenders of the struggling religion against the attacks of the official hierarchy. With such a record before them the hope of Christianity being one day established as the national faith may easily assume a concrete shape in the minds of the foreign missionaries. Perhaps it is the dream of some and the ambition of others that Christianity may once again secure a footing in the Imperial palace. One emperor, indeed, of the present dynasty has already tantalized the propaganda with delusive hopes, standing near the baptismal font, but intending only to deceive the missionaries. Members of his family were actually converted, and in the persecution which ensued on the death of

Kang-hsi the first and greatest victims were the princes and princesses of the imperial house. One was said, indeed, to have stood very near the throne, perhaps too near, for Oriental autocrats do not relish in their sight too many eligible successors, and it is not altogether incredible that the virulence with which Yung-cheng pursued the Christians was inspired by the jealousy which he naturally felt of his own brothers and their conversion was perhaps the only pretext under which he could lay hands on them.[1]   A century before the reign of Yung-cheng, a Chinese Constantine and an Empress Helena were baptized, the forlorn hope of the Mings in Kwangsi. The time may come when an actual occupant of the Dragon Throne may take the plunge. But in the interest alike of Christian progress and national peace it is to be hoped the consummation of such hopes may be deferred, long enough at least to allow Christianity to have first rooted itself in the country

[1] "The Jesuits in Peking joined a plot to supplant this emperor by a younger brother."—Rev. J. Ross, *Chinese Recorder*, August, 1892.

by the force of its own principles.[1] A Christian Emperor would be a doubtful blessing whether he were a mere political convert like Constantine, or a religious Fury like Saint Louis, or some Taiping Wang with a passion for putting nonconformists to the sword.   In any of the cases that can be conceived, the consequences almost certainly would be what they have always been, the fanatics and the quacks, even though in a small minority, ruling the Church, importing into their administration of it all the time-worn abuses, each section serving its own turn by abetting the schemes of the others.[2] The fanatics, from the moment of their obtain-

[1] "In the Christianizing of Britain the work uniformly began with the King and nobles, and from them worked down to the lower classes, instead of leavening first the people and finally reaching the King. . . . This explains the ease with which the profession of Christianity could be made or unmade at the pleasure of the ruling sovereign, and explains also how the grossest heathenism could linger long after the leaders of the nation had been baptized." — Rev. H. KINGMAN, in *Chinese Recorder*, September, 1892.

[2] "To all movements, wise or foolish, flock the two classes of follower, the sincerely convinced and the insincerely affiliated; those who think they are establishing the law of righteousness on this earth, and those who see nothing but their own advantage." — Mrs. LYNN LINTON, *Nineteenth Century*, March, 1882.

ing the power, would turn on those sects which they might deem heretical and crush them by the aid of the politicians, who would care for none of these things. And like the persecution of dissidents and unbelievers in Europe and Western Asia the oppression of Chinese by Chinese under an orthodox empire might even exceed that inflicted under a heathen *régime*. A nation thus rent by religious faction, or dominated by a religious party would be a sorry result of Christian effort. Yet even that is one of the conceivable dangers ahead, remote as it may now appear.

Such gruesome speculations may evoke protests, and the pure principles of modern Christianity combined with the refinement of the twentieth century may be appealed to as guaranty of a reign of peace and charity under any possible Christian rule. But there is no sort of ground for believing that China will begin her Christian development just at the point which Europe has reached after 1900 years of conflict; and the principles of modern Christianity are not purer than those of the primitive Church, which no sooner combined with the

passions of men than disturbances resulted
which have never entirely subsided. The religion has to assimilate in China, as elsewhere,
the local worship, mythologies, popular superstitions, — modifying them perhaps out of
recognition. It has to absorb, and eventually
to transmute, dormant passions of an order
low, but of torrential force when excited, as we
have seen, the ultimate resultant being beyond
human calculation. Organisms which have
maintained a measured and regulated life in
regions where they have been long acclimatized are apt to develop unsuspected en-
ergies when transplanted to new situations. So
perhaps it may be with the Christianity which
is hereafter to cover China; no one can foresee
how it will modify and be modified by its en-
vironment, nor toward which of the existing
forms it may approximate. Until therefore
the religion has established itself in the common life of the people[1] its professors may well
deprecate its adoption by the State. Converts
are not often made to Christianity in the ab-

---

[1] " The gospel should first strike root in the hearts of simple-
minded persons who receive it for what it is." — Dr. FABER.

stract,[1] but to some branch or section of the Church. Which? let them ask themselves who may be tempted to pray for an imperial proselyte, and a national Church.

There remains a present and practical point of contact between the Imperial Throne and the propagation of Christianity, which is sometimes alluded to by the foreign press. In the Sacred Edict, or series of Homilies instituted by the Emperor K'ang-hsi and amplified by his successors, and appointed to be publicly read twice a month in all the cities of the empire (in imitation, it is supposed, of the preaching of the early missionaries) there is an article which animadverts on the tenets of Christianity and warns the people against that religion. With a superficial show of reason, this is claimed by some foreign missionaries to be in contradiction to the toleration clauses in the various foreign treaties. But the point is of dubious validity. In the first place a doctrinal admonition is not an incentive to violence; nor is the toleration of Christianity

[1] President Lincoln, a profoundly religious man, attached himself to no Church.

inconsistent with opposing it by argument.
In the second place the passage in the Sacred
Edict should be taken in its practical rather
than in its theoretical bearing. For an Emperor deliberately to rescind the solemn enact-
ment of a revered ancestor would be a very
extreme measure; to expunge even a section
would be a serious matter. It is in fact never
done. The Chinese Emperors are as careful
not to run counter to the public acts of their
predecessors [1] as the Popes are to maintain at
least apparent harmony in their successive
Bulls; and in cases where a reversal of policy
may become a State necessity, the most con-
summate skill in the manipulation of phrases,
with a view to keeping up the semblance of
consistency, is called into play, as well in
Peking as in Rome. It appears however the
officials of their own accord discovered a *via
media* by which the susceptibilities of the foreigner were spared, for as Dr. Edkins relates
in his work on " Religion in China," the

---

[1] This is fully recognized in the temperate letter from the
Evangelical Alliance in Shanghai to H. E. Mr. Von Brandt,
Doyen of the Diplomatic body. — *Messenger*, April, 1892.

Town-Clerk of Shanghai, as probably in other places where there were foreigners, simply omitted the objectionable clause in his fortnightly reading. Like the Commination service and the Athanasian Creed in many English churches, it was treated as an anachronism, and allowed quietly to drop.

The animus of the Edict becomes further attenuated when the reference to Christianity is taken in connection with similar reflections on Taoism and Buddhism, the idolatrous practices of which are held up to the people as matters to be shunned. For the emperor who propounded the Edict himself openly patronized the Buddhists, as his successors have done on several marked public occasions. Indeed the Lama government of Tibet which the Emperors had no choice but to support, providing large establishments for the worship and residence of the priests within and without the walls of Peking itself, would have made any real opposition to Buddhism on the part of the Emperors somewhat ridiculous.

It has been shown, however, by Dr. Griffith John that the article in the Sacred Edict is

appropriated by the Hunan pamphleteers as a
base for their calumnies, and as the justification
of the outrages to which they incite the people.
And he therefore claims the rescission of the
passage in chapter seven of the *Shêng-yü* which
has been so used. "The expunging of this
one passage . . . would do more than anything else," etc.

This is not, however, the first time in religious history that atrocities have been justified
by the misuse of sacred texts, yet it has never
been proposed that the passages so used should
be forthwith expunged from the Canon. The
condemnation of those who had dared so to
pervert the sense of the Sacred Edict[1] would
probably have been in this case a more feasible
thing to demand and a simpler thing for the
government to grant.

[1] "It is not the first time that superstitious and rancorous
fanaticism has quoted respectable, and even really sacred writings
in its favor . . . I hope it is not too late to plead that the grave,
and on the whole reasonable edict may not be associated by any
but the Hunan criminals with their foul productions." —*Bishop
Moule.*

XII.

ADMINISTRATIVE MACHINERY.

THE Reformatory proposals of this character which are freely thrown out by foreigners
on all sides for the guidance of the Chinese
government, seem to be after all quite anoma-
lous. The whole practice of foreign agents
tinkering at details of internal administration
needs reconsidering. The circumstances of
China and the passive temper of the government have admitted far more of this kind of
interference than would be tolerated in any
other country, but the results have scarcely
justified the departure from orthodox usage,
and some more effective remedy should, if
possible, be devised.

Treaties were forced on the empire engaging
it to new and unknown obligations. As
regards one class of these, the commercial
stipulations, much care was taken on both

sides to provide machinery whereby the treaty provisions could be put in force smoothly, and a body of "Trade Regulations" far more elaborate than the treaties themselves, and of equal authority, were drawn up by competent officials. If such precautions were necessary with regard to a matter so clear and intelligible as commerce, how much more was it necessary to provide for the operations of religious propagandism respecting which it was quite certain that there was no common intelligence between the parties! Yet the sweeping clause granting religious toleration once inserted in the treaties, the negotiators seem to have given no further thought to the matter, leaving the practical solution of the question to be the sport of accident. The Rev. G. T. Candlin, in a letter to the *Manchester Guardian*, has pointed out this defect in a very lucid manner, and he attributes much of the missionary troubles to that very cause. No consideration whatever was shown to the Chinese government which, ignorant of the plans by which the propaganda intended to fulfil this part of the treaty, was left to discover them gradually by the collis-

ions between the evangelists and the officials
and people. It was as if the British Parlia-
ment were to vote Home Rule for Ireland,
and leave Orangemen and Catholics to work
out the details in the streets.

Take for illustration the single item of the
acquisition of sites and construction of buildings, the acknowledged source of three-fourths
of all the missionary disturbances in China.
At the Treaty ports where foreign consular
agencies are maintained in effective activity, the
most minute precautions are prescribed by
authority with a view to the prevention of
friction between foreigners and natives. The
Consul has to be a party to negotiations for the
purchase of ground, has to approve of every
step, and to investigate if there be any secret
impediments to the transfer to the foreign
buyer. After completion of the transaction
the title deeds issued by the local Chinese
authority have to be deposited with the Consul who retains control of all subsequent trans-
fers. Every safeguard is thus provided against
disputes in places where communities of foreigners and natives have learned through the

daily intercourse of life to tolerate each other, and where therefore the dangers arising from misunderstandings are but slight.

But in the interior of the country, several weeks' journey from any consul, where there is nothing but raw inflammable material on one side and zealous men, perhaps undisciplined in the common affairs of life, on the other, not only are no proper regulations provided for the aquisition of property, but even the legal rights of the missionaries are left without any authoritative definition. One half of them in fact proceed on one theory of their legal status under treaty, and the other on another, with none to guide them in their interpretation of state documents which may be inconsistent with each other; and they are left to discover, perhaps by the light of their burning houses, those hidden flaws in the tenure of ground which at a treaty port would have been ascertained for them by their Consul before the consummation of the purchase.

Chinese officials, perplexed by the uncertainties of these proceedings, are sometimes tempted to seek an illegitimate remedy by making in particular localities rules which are one-sided and unworkable. Foreign critics, perceiving the offence more clearly than the provocation, denounce such tentative regulations as subtle devices to hinder missionary work. And though no doubt such would be in many cases their effect, it would be fairer to consider them as in their inception a protest against certain defects in the international arrangements, for which the foreign treaty powers are chiefly responsible.

And even when explosions have occurred the foreign governments instead of taking the whole question seriously in hand and endeavouring to concert with the Chinese government a working scheme whereby missionaries and people might co-exist in peace have been content with spasms of recriminations and occasional interferences with the administration. There was a specific always ready for each new outbreak, and simply by forcing such and such a measure on the Chinese the foreign ministers flattered themselves that they were laying the ghost of missionary trouble. At one time it might be some proclamation or the placarding of treaties that was to have the magic effect of settling everything; at another an Edict was insisted on; and yet, again, the partial abrogation of some older Edict; or the arrest and punishment of an individual man, or the personal visitation of foreign officials to the scene. On one special occasion — unconnected, however, with Christian troubles — the government was superseded in its functions by an itinerant judicial commission composed of the nominees of a foreign Minister who imagined he could thereby elicit information in the remote interior which official efforts combined to conceal from him. All such devices imposed by foreigners were of course easily rendered nugatory by the ostensible compliance but secret frustration of the government.[1] In a country, too, where false

---

[1] "In the proclamations put out under foreign pressure the *animus* was perceptible to all who could read between the lines. . . . So evident was it that the proclamation of August 30th [in Canton] had caused the riots that one of the Consuls at least, plainly told the Viceroy so, and the Chinese generally admit that the issuing of this paper was a grave mistake." — Rev. R. H. Graves.

"Such a proclamation would have had no more effect in

accusation has been elaborated into a fine art it were futile to rely on the text of official papers for protection. All the Christians in China might be persecuted to death without a single allegation against them respecting their religion. The memorial of Kiying in 1844, which heralded the new era of toleration, is based on the alleged continuity of the imperial policy, which had never interdicted the Christian religion, though it had punished persons accused of criminal practices, who happened to be Christians.[1] A Chinese official who is degraded, and deserves it, is rarely charged with the real offence, but some other, often far-fetched, delinquencies are trumped up

Macedonia than so many dozens of them have had in China."— Dr. FABER, *Paul*.

"It is a common custom for the Court of Peking to issue double sets of instructions for the provincial governors. One set, appearing in the *Gazette*, is intended for the eye of the foreign ministers . . . but it is the other set which represents the real policy of the government." — *Shanghai and Hankow Committee of Evangelical Alliance*, 1885.

[1] The systematic duplicity is well exposed in a publication by the late Peng Yu-lin, which has recently been translated under the title of " Indulgent Treatment of Foreigners," and issued from the office of the *Shanghai Mercury*. It is a most important contribution to the elucidation of these questions.

against him. No doubt there may be valid reasons for this oblique manner of proceeding, as, for instance, that the real charge might implicate third parties whom it was not desired to censure; but at any rate the practice is consecrated by immemorial usage, and the Christians have no ground for expecting immunity from its operation. None of these empirical remedies in fact ever have had the desired effect on the relations between the people and the missionaries, and the suggestive faculties of the foreign officials have been exhausted without result.

The problem was in truth much too deep to be solved in any such perfunctory manner, and obviously the foreign ministers ought either to have dug down to the roots of the question, or treated it in quite another fashion, for their fitful interferences and nerveless discussions have only served to relieve the Chinese government of much of its moral responsibility for the execution of the treaties. The Treaty Powers ought in fact still to make good their great omission, and in concert with China, draw up " Missionary Regulations " as they did Trade Regulations thirty-four years ago.

But what would have been easy if done at the proper time would not be so now, owing to the accumulated difficulties which invariably close in over neglected opportunities.[1]　A combination of the foreign powers would seem to be essential to the drafting of any general scheme, but unfortunately there is no agreement among them, and as far as present appearances indicate there is no near prospect of any.　When the treaties were made there was practical harmony between the only powers then represented, and whatever they might have established would have bound all subsequent treaty-makers.[2]　Then, the thirty-four years

[1] On the other hand, however, the thirty years' experience of legalized missionary work has furnished *data* for practical rules of intercourse which could hardly have been anticipated by the original negotiators of treaties. The conditions of travel and residence might now be more intelligently defined, and the passport system — to specify one item — so far modified as to confer the status of permanent resident on missionaries who are now officially recognized only as travellers in the country.

[2] It should be remembered, to the credit of the statesmanship of Lord Elgin, that when negotiating the English Treaty he restrained himself from extorting concessions from China which in time to come might be taken undue advantage of, under their most-favoured-nation clauses, by Powers which having taken no part in the opening of the country, might be less sensible of responsibility than the original Treaty powers.

years which have elapsed since Christianity was legalized and left to pursue its way in China, while they have been fruitful in valuable experience have also given time for the growth of such irritation among officials and people as to embitter intercourse between them and the foreign and native Christians. The situation has consequently become so complicated that a bold initiative seems to be required from one quarter or another to restore a working equilibrium. The foreign powers, however, not only abstain from taking such initiative, but give a freezing reception to tentative proposals emanating from the Chinese government. The Memorandum of 1871 [1] remains, with all its faults, the only attempt as yet made to bring about an amicable agreement, and the Powers to whom it was addressed have neither discussed it nor made any counter-proposals of their own.

If, however, the foreign governments, from whatever cause, refuse to assist in the elaboration of a scheme of missionary relations, their

---

[1] As this state paper is often referred to and is not always accessible, it is given *in extenso*, as Appendix II.

safest alternative would be to leave the details of internal administration alone, and simply to insist on every Treaty engagement being fulfilled to the letter, letting the Chinese find for themselves the *modus operandi*. It is a recognized principle in international affairs that domestic legislation is overruled by Treaty obligations, and where there is inconsistency between the two, it rests with the government in fault to accommodate its internal machinery to its external engagements in the way most convenient to itself. The other party merely holds to the Treaty and requires its fulfilment, refusing to discuss the mechanism of administrative economy, which it could never in any case understand.

XIII.

MUTUAL OBLIGATIONS.

THE government and the literary classes of China are, as we have seen, engaged in a contest, sometimes secret, sometimes open, with a spiritual force whose true nature they understand less than they do the nature of electricity; a force which would gladly live on good terms with them, but which, in any case, will live with, and probably after, them.

Their objections to the Western religion, whether well or ill-founded, can in no wise be allowed, for Christianity will not be denied entrance, no matter what obstacles be opposed to it.

The Western governments, on the other hand, which broke down the Chinese wall and, by right of conquest, compelled the nation to receive foreign missionaries, were, and are, morally bound to assist the government of

China to devise means whereby the unwelcome
religion may be admitted with the minimum of
friction ; but they evade the obligation.   Neither, indeed, could they fulfil it if they would,
without such union among themselves as, under existing circumstances, seems unattainable.
For a moment's reflection on the respective
positions of the Great Powers is sufficient to
show the unlikelihood of any steady concerted
action among them.   Though in national
concerns nice scruples have to give way to im-
perious interests, there still exists something in
the nature of a public conscience to whose re-
quirements the most powerful states pay at
least a formal deference.   More than one of
the Powers having relations with China would
find their hands somewhat tied by considerations of this kind.   What sincerity, for example, might Russia be expected to throw into
any scheme of forcible protection of a propaganda in China, which at home she utterly
prohibits?   Anti-clerical France, which subordinates her interest, even in the Catholic missions, to her other ends could never be relied
on to support in China those Protestant mis-

sions which she expels from her African do-
minions. How, again, could the United
States join in pressing China to receive and
protect either American or other missionaries
while, in the face of treaty engagements, they
refuse standing room for Chinese on their
wide territory? And Spain — what figure
would she make as the Defender of the British
and Foreign Bible Society? There would remain of course Great Britain, Germany, and
Italy, catholic and comparatively clean-handed,
who might act together with a tolerably easy
conscience. But is it quite sure that such
a triple alliance would be allowed by the ab-
stinents a free hand to protect Christianity in
China? Experience seems rather against such
a supposition. The concert of the Powers,
therefore, appears to be little more than a
diplomatic platitude, and viewed in this light,
the armed forces of Christendom have conferred on Christianity in China only a compro-
mising alliance while leaving it, in the stress of
conflict, to the mercy of exasperated foes, yet
ready nevertheless to step in, in the last resort,
to avenge some ideal atrocity.

Common action therefore seems out of the question, and without common action on the part of foreign powers no ordinances of the Chinese could take effect, because the missions belong to various nationalities, and none of them would respect rules not sanctioned by their own representatives, while separate rules for each would be entirely unworkable.

The Powers may, of course, cut the Gordian knot with the sword, as has been done more than once; and if they, or even any one of them, would but consistently apply this method the question might soon be solved and set at rest. For the officials, scholars, and people, once compelled to respect and protect Christians without chance of evasion, would become habituated to the forms of toleration, and might in time learn to practise voluntarily what they had been trained to do by force. But enforced toleration — almost a contradiction in terms — to be effective would admit of no exceptions and no wavering. Conciliation may be good, and compulsion may be good; but the oscillation between the two is nearly certain to fail,

because, for one thing, the alternating phases
would be pretty certain to be exhibited at the
least appropriate times.

Failing, then, assistance from foreign governments or their representatives, the Chinese
rulers are thrown back on their own resources
to discover a *modus vivendi* between their
people and the promiscuous elements, foreign
and native, which make up the Propaganda.
These resources are inadequate to the task:
first, because of the inexperience of Chinese
statesmen and their non-comprehension of the
character of Christianity; and secondly, on
account of their preconceived antipathy, latent
and active by turns, to the religion, and their repugnance to all candid examination of it. This
characteristic must paralyze, by tainting with
insincerity, any unaided efforts of Government
to devise a basis of agreement with the propaganda. Notwithstanding these disqualifica-
tions, however, the Chinese government cannot
escape the necessity of dealing with this grave
question, though its action in regard to it
seems, by the very nature of the case, fore-

doomed to barrenness. For the evasive policy of the government opposed to the more consistent tactics of the propaganda must produce continuous friction, generating heat, and leading, not seldom, to explosions.

It would almost appear, therefore, that the conflict, like a biological ferment, must run its course without any intelligent direction from the parties principally concerned; and, if the history of the invasion of Buddhism may be taken as a precedent, centuries of strife may have to be waded through before the struggle can issue in settled peace.

But as in the most desperate condition of any State there are still individuals "who do not despair of the republic," but are animated with courage even to resist fate, so there may not be wanting in China statesmen who, in spite of adverse circumstances, will do their best to smooth the way for the accommodation of Christianity in this country, some from motives of temporary expediency, and some, perhaps, from an awakening conviction of the blessings which the religion, notwithstanding the faults of its propagators, has to offer them.

The light cannot for ever be excluded, however resolutely men may close their eyes against it; and in time one and another, even of the Chinese *literati*, many of whom are now seriously inquiring into its merits, must be able, as in the days gone by, to appreciate Christianity. To suppose otherwise indeed were to concede it to be the imposture which the *literati* as a body now affect to regard it.

But while the Western governments stand paralysed by disunion and conflicting interests, and the Chinese government and governing classes are floundering in the dark, there is an important third party, the propaganda itself, which being endued with light as well as heat, ought to play an effective part in the solution of the religious question in China. Being *primâ facie* responsible for the existence of the trouble the onus rests peculiarly on the missions to send a peaceful issue out of the *imbroglio*, and to find some broader ground to stand on than that of mere contention for the uttermost rights conferred on them by the letter of

the treaties.[1]   The case is not uncommon in
the Western hemisphere where laws made in
advance of the opinion of the community [2] cannot be enforced without violence, and where
the beneficiaries, realizing this, submit to the
waiving of rights which have been definitively
secured to them by statute.

The pretensions of foreign missions in China
are of such a nature as to entail upon them an
exceptional degree of moral responsibility for
the consequences of their action; and from
which shelter is not to be found within the four
corners of any legal instrument whatsoever.
For they assume authority, without appeal,
over the minds and consciences of millions of
human beings; they claim absolute superiority
over the long line of teachers and moralists
who have preceded them in China: they exer-

[1] " Such forcing, based on treaty rights, maintained by much
disagreeable correspondence between foreign consuls and Chinese
high mandarins, has done a great deal to shut up the hearts of
the people against the Gospel." — DR. FABER.

[2] " You cannot have that steady, firm, consistent administration of the law permanently established until you have brought
the provisions of the law and the sympathies of the people into
harmony." — MR. GLADSTONE in House of Commons, August
9th, 1892.

cise, without reserve, the prerogative of eradi-
cation of all customs, religions, and worships
which they disapprove, under a divine mandate
attested by themselves. From such an order
of men it were surely not unreasonable to look
for some with capacity to manage this perplexing question without constant explosions and
appeals to brute force. Force implies failure
in almost all the circumstances of life where
resort to it is necessary ; and the Christian
mission bodies owe it to their own cause and
character to show that they are at least not ob-
livious of the high qualities which their self-
assumed position requires of them.

Christian societies in sending out missionaries
do not thereby discharge, but incur, obligations
of the gravest character. The evangelization
of China is not the simple numerical problem
it is often assumed to be, and long lists of
missionaries and columns of subscriptions are
of themselves no true cause for gratulation.
If the parent bodies weighed their own respon-
sibilities conscientiously they would rank the
quality of mere fervour somewhat low, and
would choose their agents rather for their

liberality of education and temperament, their
catholic human sympathies, their common sense,
their aptitude to learn from observation and
experience, and their freedom from dogmatic
assurance. The office of missionary to a people
like the Chinese demands exceptional gifts, and
the ranks cannot be filled from the waifs and
strays of religious life without endangering the
whole enterprise. One man of the right stamp
is worth a thousand impatient zealots, who
accomplish no permanent good themselves, and
by their indiscretions destroy the influence of
those who work on a sounder basis.

Happily this sense of responsibility seems
to be spreading in missionary circles. There
have been, and are, serious men in the various
missions who cannot shut their eyes to the
light of the world, and there are some who,
especially in their declining years, question
themselves deeply concerning the manner and
results of their life's labours, and cast about
earnestly for some more excellent way, if by
any means discoverable. Such an one, it may
now be said without impropriety, was the late
Dr. Williamson who sunk to rest only two

years ago. And there is probably an increasing number who instinctively look first for faults on their own side, whose feelings towards the shortcomings of the Chinese are something more humane than pity and more Christian than contempt. Since the foregoing pages were written there has appeared an essay by a worthy follower of Dr. Williamson, the Rev. G. Candlin, reprinted in *Chinese Recorder* for March, 1892, in which the tactics of provocation and mere destructive attack on native beliefs and institutions is shown to be by no means the most effective way of transforming them. The welcome of such a candid deliverance by the editors of a mission organ proves that the reasonable school is gaining courage, and seems like the dawn of a brighter day. From the extension of such a school there would be much to hope, both for the progress of Christianity itself, and also for its peaceful contact with the official and lettered classes.[1]

The whole history of missions testifies that there is no personal sacrifice or bodily risk

[1] See also a courageous and straightforward paper by the Rev. J. Ross, of Moukden, in *Chinese Recorder*, August, 1892.

which Christian teachers would not incur for
the sake of the propagation of their faith.   In
order to free their cause from its political associations many would willingly forego the protection of their own governments ; some would
go further, and divesting themselves of their
birthright, would cheerfully accept the full conditions of Chinese nationality.   Such ideas of
course can never be more than pious aspirations, for the protection extended by civilized
states to their citizens, being based on the
interest of the whole community, cannot be
switched on and off, like an electric light, by
individual caprice.   Still less is it within the
competence of any one to exempt himself by a
private resolution from the obligations inherent
in his nationality.   As his government would
remain responsible for him he would still be
answerable to his government.   And were
even the detachment from country and kin-
dred legally effected the missionary would still
not have attained his object, for no metempsy-
chosis could undo his origin and lineage.   He
would remain essentially the alien, though
stripped of the privileges and abjuring the pre-

tensions appertaining to an extra-territorialized foreigner. And ten-to-one but the Chinese would see in his renunciation only a more unfathomable depth of cunning.

But if willing to do the "great thing" which is not required of them, the mission leaders should also be, as no doubt they are, ready to promote less heroic measures for the improvement of the situation. Were it possible to bring the parties together on some neutral platform where a dispassionate interchange of views might take place between moderate and reasonable men selected from both sides, such a conference would not perhaps be wholly barren of result. Assuming that there is no radical incapacity on either side for appreciating the position of the other, and presuming peace to be the common object, an earnest effort to secure it, even if but partially successful in its specific aim, could hardly fail to achieve something in the direction of a mutual understanding. And any *rapprochement* which would admit of the Christian propaganda being carried on with fewer of those violent concussions which have hitherto marked its advance would be an object well worthy of such efforts.

The obstacles in the way of organizing any kind of deliberative concourse are formidable and obvious. For the Chinese it would be a revolutionary innovation on their traditional methods of procedure; and for a mixed body composed of numerous independent members like the foreign Missions it would not be a very simple matter to concentrate effective authority on any selected representatives. The difficulty of arriving at such an understanding is naturally greatly diminished in the case of the Catholic section of the propaganda, where the representative apparatus already exists in a highly organized form. Other hope failing, therefore, it seems to be after all to the Vatican and its disciplined agents that the Christian world will have to look, if anywhere, for extrication from its dilemma in China; for, having been repulsed elsewhere, it is to that quarter that the Imperial government would naturally address itself, if the personal and national schemes of foreign diplomatists would but permit it so much liberty of action.

To discuss the terms of a possible Concordat, whether partial or general, while as yet the steps preliminary to any agreement whatever cannot be marked out would be altogether premature. Much ground has to be gone over, even under the most favourable circumstances, before the desired composition of differences can be brought within the sphere of practical politics.

Should it eventually be demonstrated that reconciliation between the parties is unattainable it would nevertheless be a real gain even to ascertain that much, so that the air might be cleared of distracting illusions. The Christian propaganda would then be able to continue the contest with China on definite conditions, and China would know better what it had to deal with. It may be that the actual struggle for existence is as essential an element in the evolution of religious systems as it is in that of other forms of life, and that all attempts to evade its hard conditions are but amiable weaknesses? Left alone with its Pagan antagonists Christianity would no doubt in the end fight its way to victory; although the re-

markable collapse of the missions in High
Asia, after a fierce conflict sustained for many
centuries by an energy which can never be
surpassed, and the extinction of mediæval
Christianity in China proper by religions much
inferior to itself, stand as warnings to the propaganda that ultimate triumph, though sure, may
have to be purchased dearly, and may be long
deferred.

As for the Chinese government, its neglect-
ing the opportunity of "agreeing with its adversary" would be only too much in keeping
with its general *laissez-faire* policy, which per-
mits destructive inundations, famines, insur-
rections to devastate the country, without
prevision or precaution on any adequate scale,
and which conducts its external relations in
such a negligent manner as continually to in-
vite territorial aggression.

In conclusion, let not the inadequacy of the
treatment obscure the greatness of the subject.
For, above all the local friction, ephemeral
disputation and political veering and hauling;
above the shiftiness of some and the intensity
of others, above the fret and fuss of the day's

work, we really stand in the presence of one
of those grand cosmic conjunctures which shape
human destinies. It is one half of the world
which is challenging the other half; all Christendom gathering its strength to subdue all
Paganism. Each of them is strong by what
there is in it of truth and nobleness, while our
judgment is bewildered by the error and prejudice which cling to them both; and if the
very term we are compelled by the infirmity of
our language to employ to mark their antithesis
seems to beg the question as to their relative
merits, it is but a nickname which may be
balanced by the coinage of some equally dis-
paraging term on the other side. Both forces
are majestic in their wide and enduring sway
over the hearts of men, in their impulse to
virtue, in sustaining the human spirit in its
struggle for light. None of the historic conflicts of the race, though carried on with clamour
and bloodshed, have been laden with vaster
issues; for this, in its true essence, is a contest
of mind against mind. The whole life and
growth and morality, linked together throughout long ages, of the largest human society the

Sun ever looked upon, actually circulating in the blood of the living men of to-day, — this entity which we call China — is invited, nay, summoned, to surrender much that, in its own opinion, has immortalized the nation. View it how we may, and with all possible deductions, the grandeur of a people who have come through the stages of human development not only intact, but expanding and unified, who have made magnificent attempts to solve the mystery of the Unseen, and who have distilled out of their philosophical speculations a system of practical ethics which has served them, without revision, for more than two thousand years — must command the homage of civilized men.

On the other hand, the forces opposed to it have also their history and their rich experiences. The leaven which has worked in the Western races, inspiring their greatest achievements and imbuing them with the principle of *extension* and *advancement* works still with unabated energy. It is that vital principle which after many centuries of effort, has at length brought the forces of Christendom to the gates of the East, where, with or without ceremony, they demand admittance. With all reasonable qualifications, Christendom is probably not too arrogant in claiming for itself pre-eminence among the families of man.

We who live near the very meeting points of the two powers can only by a mental effort dimly conceive the magnitude of the issues which are being worked out under our eyes. Where is the MAN who can understand the epoch, blend the opposing currents into wholesome and vital union, guide them into safe and fruitful channels; and from the blackening sky conduct the storm-fluid innocuously to earth?

APPENDIX I.

❧

MEMORIAL OF IMPERIAL COMMISSIONER KÍYING, 1844.

KÍYING, imperial commissioner, minister of State, and governor-general of Kwangtung and Kwangsi, respectfully addresses the throne by memorial.

On examination it appears that the religion of the Lord of Heaven is that professed by all the nations of the West; that its main object is to encourage the good and suppress the wicked; that since its introduction to China during the Ming dynasty it has never been interdicted; that subsequently, when Chinese, practising this religion, often made it a covert for wickedness, even to the seducing of wives and daughters, and to the deceitful extraction of the pupils from the eyes of the sick, government made investigation and in-

flicted punishment, as is on record; and that
in the reign of Kiaking special clauses were
first laid down for the punishment of the
guilty. The prohibition, therefore, was di-
rected against evil-doing under the covert of
religion, and not against the religion professed
by the western foreign nations.

Now the request of the French ambassador,
Lagrené, that those Chinese who, doing well,
practise this religion, be exempt from criminality, seems feasible. It is right, therefore,
to make the request, and earnestly to crave
celestial favour to grant that, henceforth, all
natives and foreigners without distinction,
who learn and practice the religion of the
Lord of Heaven, and do not excite trouble
by improper conduct, be exempted from criminality. If there be any who seduce wives
and daughters, or deceitfully take the pupils
from the eyes of the sick, walking in their
former paths, or are otherwise guilty of criminal acts, let them be dealt with according to
the old laws. As to those of the French and
other foreign nations who practise the religion,
let them only be permitted to build churches

at the five ports opened for commercial intercourse. They must not presume to enter the country to propagate religion. Should any act in opposition, turn their backs upon the treaties, and rashly overstep the boundaries, the local officers will at once seize and deliver them to their respective consuls for restraint and correction. Capital punishment is not to be rashly inflicted, in order that the exercise of gentleness must be displayed. Thus, peradventure, the good and the profligate will not be blended, while the equity of mild laws will be exhibited.

This request, that well-doers practising the religion may be exempt from criminality, I (the commissioner), in accordance with reason and bounden duty, respectfully lay before the throne, earnestly praying the august Emperor graciously to grant that it may be carried into effect. A respectful memorial.

Taukwang, 24th year, 11th month, 19th day (December 28, 1844), was received the vermilion reply: "Let it be according to the counsel [of Kíying]." This is from the Emperor.

Second Memorial of Kíying, 1845.

Now I find that, in the first place, when the regulations for free trade were agreed upon, there was an article allowing the erection of churches at the five ports. This same privilege was to extend to all nations; there were to be no distinctions. Subsequently the commissioner Lagrené requested that the Chinese who, acting well, practised this religion, should equally be held blameless. Accordingly, I made a representation of the case to the throne, by memorial, and received the imperial consent thereto. After this, however, local magistrates having made improper seizures, taking and destroying crosses, pictures, and images, further deliberations were held, and it was agreed that these [crosses, etc.] might be reverenced. Originally I did not know that there were, among the nations, these differences in their religious practices. Now with regard to the religion of the Lord of Heaven — no matter whether the crosses, pictures, and images be reverenced or be not reverenced — all who, acting well, practise it, ought to be held blameless. All the great western nations being placed on an equal footing, only let them be acting well, practise their religion, and China will in no way prohibit or impede their so doing. Whether their customs be alike or unlike, certainly it is right and there should be no distinction and no obstruction. — *December* 22, 1845.

Imperial Rescript on Above.

On a former occasion Kíying and others laid before Us a memorial, requesting immunity from punishment for those who doing well profess the religion of Heaven's Lord; and that those who erect churches, assemble together for worship, venerate the cross and pictures and images, read and explain sacred books, be not prohibited from so doing. This was granted. The religion of the Lord of Heaven, instructing and guiding men in well-doing, differs widely from the heterodox and illicit sects; and the toleration thereof has already been allowed. That which has been requested

on a subsequent occasion, it is right in like
manner to grant.

Let all the ancient houses throughout the
provinces, which were built in the reign of
Kanghi, and have been preserved to the present time, and which, on personal examination
by proper authorities, are clearly found to be
their *bona fide* possessions, be restored to the
professors of this religion in their respective
places, excepting only those churches which
have been converted into temples and dwelling-
houses for the people.

If, after the promulgation of this decree
throughout the provinces, the local officers ir-
regularly prosecute and seize any of the professors of the religion of the Lord of Heaven,
who are not bandits, upon all such the just
penalties of the law shall be meted out.

If any, under a profession of this religion,
do evil, or congregate people from distant
towns, seducing and binding them together; or
if any other sect or bandits, borrowing the
name of the religion of the Lord of Heaven,
create disturbances, transgress the laws, or excite rebellion, they shall be punished according

to their respective crimes, each being dealt with as the existing statutes of the Empire direct.

Also, in order to make apparent the proper distinctions, foreigners of every nation are, in accordance with existing regulations, prohibited from going into the country to propagate religion.

For these purposes this decree is given. Cause it to be made known.   From the Emperor.

APPENDIX II.

꙰

CIRCULAR OF THE CHINESE GOVERN-MENT, 1871.

(COMMUNICATED BY THE FRENCH CHARGÉ D'AFFAIRES.)

Translation.

THE object which the Powers and China had before them originally in signing the treaties was to establish a permanent situation which should ensure them reciprocal advantages and remove abuses. However, the experience of the last few years has demonstrated that not only do these Treaties not attain this desired end of permanency, but also that, up to the present time, they are difficult to carry into execution. Trade has in no degree occasioned differences between China and the Powers. The same cannot be said of the missions, which engender ever increasing abuses. Al-

though in the first instance it may have been
declared that the primary object of the missions
was to exhort men to virtue, Catholicism in
causing vexation to the people, has produced
a contrary effect in China. (This regrettable
result) is solely attributable to the inefficacy of
the plan of action (followed in this matter).
It is, therefore, urgent that steps should be
taken to remedy this evil, and to search for a
satisfactory solution of the difficulty. In fact,
this question is one bearing upon those which
influence the leading interests of the peace of
nations, as well those of their trade, which are
equally considerable. Wherever the Catholic
missionaries have appeared, they have drawn
upon themselves the animadversion of the
people, and your Excellency is not ignorant
that cases which have arisen during the course
of several years embraced points of disagreement of every kind.

The first Catholic Missionaries who established themselves in China were called "literates" of the West. The greater part of the
conversions took place at that time among
respectable people. On the other hand, since

the conclusion of the Treaties took place
(1860) the majority of the converts are persons
without virtue; so that religion, whose object
is to exhort men to virtue, no longer enjoys
any consideration. From that moment consciences have become a prey to uneasiness.
The Christians have none the less continued,
under the shadow of missionary influence, to
mislead and oppress the people: thence arose
renewed uneasiness, then quarrels between
Christians and non-Christians, and, at last,
disturbances. The authorities proceed to investigate the affair; the missionaries make
common cause with the Christians, and support them in their insubordination against the
same authorities. Thereupon the feeling of
disquiet which pervades the people assumes
greater proportions. Yet more: veteran
rebels, beyond the pale of the law, amateurs
in intrigue, seek a refuge in the Church, and
lean upon her influence in order to commit
disorders. At this moment the animosity of
the people, already deep, degenerates gradually
into a hate which, at length, reaches its par-
oxysm. The people in general, unaware of

the difference which exists between Protestantism and Catholicism, confound these two religions under this latter denomination. They do not grasp the distinction which should be made between the different nations of which Europe is composed, and give to Europeans the generic name of "men from without;" so that, when troubles break out, foreigners residing in China are all exposed to the same dangers. Even in the provinces where conflicts have not yet taken place uneasiness and suspicion will certainly appear among the people. Is not such a state of things of a nature to occasion a lively feeling of irritation, and, as a result, grave disorders? The difference which exists between the religions and the nationalities are truths which are still beyond the comprehension of the masses, in spite of constant efforts which have been exerted in order to make them appreciate their nature. The Prince and the members of the Yamên, during the ten years in which they have been at the head of affairs, have been a prey to incessant anxiety. These precautions have been justified by the events at Tientsin, the

suddenness of which was overwhelming. The
proceeding against the functionaries (compro-
mised) have been begun, the murderers have
suffered capital punishment, an indemnity
has been paid, and relief given; but, although the affair may to-day be almost
settled, the Prince and the members of the
Yamên cannot throw off the uneasiness which
they feel. In fact, if this policy is the only
one on which one can rely (to settle) the differences between Christians and non-Christians,
it will become more precarious in proportion
to the necessity there will be to recur to it
oftener, and disorders like those of Tientsin will
be repeated more terribly each time. If the
matter is looked at under its present aspect, the
question is, how is it possible to be on good
terms and to live on either side in peace? It
is not only to the hatred engendered by the
suppressed animosities of the people, but decidedly also to the provocations of the Christians, that the conflicts on the missionary question which arise in these provinces must be
attributed. If, on one side, these conflicts may
have been brought about by the relative in-

capacity of the local administration, they can certainly also be attributed to the conduct of the high Chinese and European functionaries charged with the direction of affairs (affecting the two countries), who, knowing the want of conciliation in the attitude of the missionaries and Christians, show no good will in seeking for the means of remedying the evil.

With regard to the Europeans, they only aim at getting rid of the difficulties of the moment, without troubling themselves, whether by so doing consciences are disturbed; to employ coercion is all that is thought of. On the other hand, the local authorities have only one object, that of bringing the matter to a close. Care for the future goes for nothing in this short-sighted policy. But if we seek, in concert with the Europeans, to secure by efficacious means a really lasting understanding, we do not find among these latter the desire to found the discussion on equitable bases. When this discussion arises, they place before us unacceptable means which they wish to impose on us by force, in order to be able to put a stop to the matter. That is, in truth, not the

good and true way to take care of the interests
of the two countries.   Anxious about the whole
matter, and sincerely desirous that concord and
peace should reign forever between China and
Europe, the Prince and the members of the
Yamên are bound to seek the best means to
secure this result.   Their belief is, that there
are ecclesiastics everywhere in Europe, and that
their presence abroad is therefore without danger to good harmony.   The maintenance of
this happy state of things is, doubtless, due to
the employment of certain means, and to the
fact that ecclesiastics and Christians abstain
from provoking conflicts. The Prince and
members of the Yamên have heard that these
same ecclesiastics, to whatever nationality they
might belong, respected the law and customs
of the country where they dwelt; that they
were not allowed to constitute in them a kind
of exceptional independence for themselves;
and that the faults of every kind, such as con-
traventions of the law, insubordination towards
the authority of functionaries, abuses and usur-
pations of powers, acts prejudicial to the reputation of the people, and oppressive towards

the people, which provoke its suspicions and
its resentment, are there severely repressed. If
the missionaries, before constructing the religious establishments in China and preaching
their doctrine there, avoided making themselves
odious to the principal men and people, the
suspicions would disappear, to give place to a
mutual confidence; concord would be permanent; one would not see churches destroyed,
and religions attacked. If these same missionaries, in pursuit of their work, could inspire in
the masses the conviction that their acts are
not opposed to their teaching; if, remaining
deaf to the instigations of the Christians, they
avoided by denying themselves all interference
in the local administration, giving the support
of their influence to arbitrary and oppressive
acts which engender hatred among the notables
and the people, they might live in perfect harmony with the people, and the functionaries
would be in a position to protect them. Far
different is the conduct of the persons who
now come to China to propagate therein the
Christian religion. From the information
which the Prince and the Yamên have gathered

(respecting the duties imposed on them by
their priesthood), these persons found as it
were among us an undetermined number of
States within the State. How, under these
conditions, can we hope that a durable understanding should be established, and to prevent
the governors and the governed uniting against
them in common hostility?

The Prince and the members of the Yamên
are impressed with a desire to ward off from
henceforth eventualities so menacing. In fact,
they fear in all sincerity lest, after the arrangement of the Tientsin affair, the animosity of
the ignorant Christians of the Empire should
take a more decided tone of insolent bluster,
that the bitterness of the popular resentment
should increase, and that so much accumulated
bad feeling, causing a sudden explosion, should
bring about a catastrophe. It would then be
no longer possible for the local authorities, nor
for the high provincial functionaries, nor even
for the Tsung-li Yamên, to assert their authority. In the event of a general rising in China,
the Emperor will be able to appoint high dig-
nitaries to order them to assemble everywhere

imposing forces; but the greatest rigour does not reach the masses, and where their anger manifests itself, there are persons who refuse to yield their heads to the executioner. Then, when the evil becomes irremediable, and when the wish we all have to preserve so great interests will no longer be effectual, the men who direct the international affairs of China and of Europe will not be suffered to decline the responsibility which falls on them. In short, in the direction of affairs, the important point in China as in Europe, is to satisfy opinion. If failing in this duty, oppression and violence are employed, a general rising will at last take place. There are moments when the supreme authority is disregarded. If the high functionaries of China and the Europeans on whom rests the responsibility of the affairs which now form the object of our anxiety, remaining unmoved spectators of a situation which threatens the greatest danger to the Chinese people, as well as to strangers, traders and individuals, make no effort to find a solution which may effectually remedy the evil, it will follow that it will be out of their power to deal in a satisfactory manner with the matters which interest the public. Consequently with the view of protecting the great interests of general peace, and of remedying the abuses above pointed out, the Prince and the Members of the Yamên have the honor to submit for your Excellency's examination, a plan of Regulation in eight Articles, which has also been communicated to the Representatives of other Powers.

DRAFT OF REGULATIONS.

ARTICLE I.

The Christians when they found an Orphanage give no notice to the authorities, and appear to act with mystery : hence the suspicions and hatred of the people. In ceasing to receive children, the evil rumours which are now in circulation would at the same time disappear. If, however, there is a wish to continue this work, only the children of necessitous Christians must be received, and then the authorities ought to be informed, who would note the day on which the child entered, the name of its parents, and the day on which it left. It would also be necessary that power should be given to strangers to adopt these children, and then a good result would be arrived at. Lastly, when it is a question of non-Christian children, the high officials ought to give orders to the local authorities, who should select proper agents who could take all the measures which appeared suitable to them.

In China the laws which regulate orphanages are: that on the entrance and on the departure of the children note is made of the person who leaves them, or of the person who adopts them, of the declaration made to the authorities, and of the permission given to the parents to visit their children. When they have become bigger, they may be adopted by someone having no children, or taken back by the parents themselves, and then no matter in what religion they have been brought up, they return to the religions of their fathers. The child ought in everything also to be treated well. In exercising this work of charity, it becomes a most worthy work.

We have heard it said that in every country matters are conducted in this respect very

nearly as in China. How does it happen that,
once arrived in our country, foreigners no longer
follow these customs? They take no note of
the family to which the child belongs, and they
do not give notice to the authorities. Once
the child has entered the house other persons
are not allowed to adopt it, nor are the parents
permitted to take it back again, nor even to
visit it. All this nourishes suspicions and excites the hatred of the people, and by degrees
a case like that of Tientsin is arrived at. Although we have denied in a report all those
rumours of the tearing out of eyes and hearts,
the people, however, still preserve doubts on
the subject, and even if we succeed in closing
their lips we cannot drive away these doubts
from their minds. It is this kind of uneasiness
which gives rise to terrible events. It would
be a good thing to abolish the foreign orphanages, and to transport them to Europe, where
they could practise their charity at their ease :
it would then belong to the Chinese to come
to the aid of these children. Besides, in every
province we have numerous orphanages, and
yet the foreigners wish to lend us at any price

an assistance of which we have not the slightest
need. It is certainly with good intentions they
thus act, but it is not the less true that their
conduct produces suspicion and excites anger.
It would be far preferable if each one exercised
his charity in his own country, and then no
lamentable event could arise:

ARTICLE 2.

Women ought no longer to enter the
churches, nor should sisters of charity live in
China to teach religion. This measure will
only render the Christians more respectable,
and will result in silencing evil rumours.

In China good reputation and modesty are
most important matters: men and women are
not even allowed to shake hands, nor to live
together: there ought to be a kind of line of
separation that cannot be overstepped. After
the treaty full liberty was given to the Christians, and then men and women went together
to church: hence rumours among the public.
There are some places even where men and
women are together not only at church but also
in the interior of the house. The public look-

ing at this in a light manner harbours suspicions, and thinks that things contrary to propriety take place.

ARTICLE 3.

The missionaries residing in China must conform to the laws and customs of China. They are not permitted to place themselves in a kind of exceptional independence, to show themselves recalcitrant to the authority of the Government and of the officials, to attribute to themselves powers which do not belong to them, to injure the reputation of men, to oppress the people, to asperse the doctrine of Confucius, by which they give ground for the suspicions, the resentments and the indignation of the masses. The missionaries must submit themselves, like everybody, to the authority of the local officials ; and the Christian Chinese must, in every case, be treated according to the common law; with the exception of the expenses of theatrical solemnities and of the worship of local protecting divinities from which they are dispensed from contributing to, the Christians cannot escape the requisitions

and forced labour, and are constrained to
accept, like everybody else, the charges imposed by the local administration.   With
stronger reason they cannot refuse to pay, in
their integrity, the land taxes and the rents,
nor can the missionaries advise them and support them in infringing the common law.
Cases for litigation between Christians and
non-Christians are under the equitable jurisdiction of the authorities, and cannot be left to
the patronage of the missionaries.   The latter
cannot keep away from the courts, Christians,
prosecutors or defendants, which, in a trial,
leads to delays and prejudices the parties interested.   In the cases in which missionaries
allow themselves to be mixed up in affairs
beyond their province, the local authorities
ought to send their verbal or written communications to the high provincial functionaries,
who will refer them in their turn to the Tsung-
li Yamên, in order that a decision may be
eventually taken as to the repatriation of these
same missionaries.   In the cases where Christians in suits respecting matrimonial alliances
or property in land plume themselves on their

position of Christians to invoke the intervention of the missionaries, they will be severely punished by the authorities.

China honours the religion of Confucius; that of Buddha and of Tao, as well as the doctrine of the Lamas is also professed there. Therefore it is contrary to usage that the latter, although they may not be Chinese, should ignore the decisions of the Chinese authorities, by approving or blaming them. We hear it said that the missionaries in foreign countries are subject to the legislation of the country in which they live, and that they are forbidden to make themselves independent, to contravene the law, to usurp authority, to attack the character of people, or to prejudice them, or to arouse the suspicion and resentment of the people. Similarly the missionaries, who teach their religion in China, ought to submit themselves to the authority of the magistrates of this country; nevertheless they are vauntingly independent and do not recognise the authority of the officials. Do they not thus place themselves without the pale of the law? The Christians in China remain Chinese subjects,

and are only the more constrained to remain
faithful to their duties. In no case can indifference be established between them and the rest
of the nation. The Christians in the towns
and in the country ought to live in good
harmony with their fellow countrymen. Yet,
in matters affecting the public when popular
subscriptions are opened or forced labour required, they put forward their position as
Christians to escape these burdens. They
themselves create an exception (in their favour).
How avoid that the rest of the nation accept
this exception (against them)? Yet more,
they refuse the taxes and forced labour, they
intimidate the officials, they oppress those who
do not belong to their religion. The foreign
missionaries do not fully understand the situation: not only do they give an asylum to
Christians who are guilty of crimes and refuse
to deliver them up to justice, but they also
consent to protect unjustly those who have
only become converts because they have committed some crime. In the provinces the
Missionaries make themselves the advocates before the local authorities of the Christians who

have suits. Witness that Christian woman of
Sze-chuen who exacted from her tenants pay-
ments of a nature which were not due to her,
and ultimately committed a murder. A French
bishop took upon himself to address a despatch
to the authorities in order to plead for this
woman and procured her acquittal. This deed
aroused animosities among the people of Sze-
chuen which have lasted to this day.   In
Kwei-chow, Christians who go to law style
themselves Christians in the charge sheet
("acte d'accusation") with the sole view of
gaining their cause. This is a well-known
abuse. It happens also that two families being
united by matrimonial ties, one is converted
to Christianity, then compels the other who is
not converted to break off the alliance.
Among people of the same blood one has
seen fathers and older brothers, after having
been converted lay an accusation for non-ful-
filment of family duties against their children
and younger brothers, for the sole reason that
these latter had refused to be converted. These
acts are encouraged by the missionaries. Are
not such practices of a nature to excite to the
highest degree the popular indignation?

ARTICLE 4.

Chinese and foreigners living together ought to be governed by the same laws. For example, if a man kills another, he ought to be punished, if a Chinaman, according to the Chinese law; if he is a foreigner, according to the law of his country. In thus acting, order will reign; it matters little the manner in which the Chinese or foreigners treat the case; a punishment is all that is necessary. But that punishment once inflicted, they must not come and claim indemnities, and above all they must not seek the *soi-disant* abettor of the crime to exact from him a certain sum. It belongs to the local authorities to adjudicate on the differences which may arise between the Christians and the people. If it is a Pagan who has committed wrongs against a Christian, he ought to be punished more or less severely, according to the gravity of the fault; similarly if it is a question of a Christian accused by a Pagan. The official ought to adjudicate with the most perfect justice, and the greatest impartiality.

If a Christian conducts himself altogether

contrary to the laws, the local authority takes evidence; and if some one accuses this Christian, the latter is seized and judged. But the missionaries must not then come forward to defend him, and to exculpate him. If the case arises of a missionary preventing a Christian giving himself up to the commands of the authority, the Christian alone ought not to be punished, but also the missionary, or at least he ought to be sent back to his own country.

In the sixth year of the reign of T'ung Chih, a missionary, M. Mabileau, was killed in Szechuen. The murderer, named Yang Lao-wu, was arrested and condemned to death. But besides that, Mr. Mihières accused a man who formed part of the class of literates of having been the instigator of that murder, in order to exact from him an indemnity of 80,000 taels.

The individuals who commit disorders ordinarily belong to the lowest classes of the people. When they are guilty of some crime, they are seized and punished; but accusations ought not to be brought against the literates to exact from them large indemnities. Such conduct excites hatred.

In the eighth year of the reign of T'ung Chih, a missionary, Mr. Rigaud, was killed in Sze-chuen; the cause of the murder was an alliance between two families, which fell through. The Tartar General Ch'ung and the Governor General Li judged this case. They caused the murderer of Mr. Rigaud to be arrested, a man named Ho-tsai, and the murderer of a Christian named Liang-fu, both belonging to the lowest class. One was condemned to have his head cut off, the other to be hanged. The Christians further killed some of the people; every year there were conflicts between creditors and debtors, rapes and fires.

The instigators of all this were Wang Hsiao-ting, Ch'ang Tien-hsing, and others. It was desired to seize and punish them, but they did not surrender themselves to the commands of the authority. Further, the Christians again, under the leadership of a priest named Tan Fu-ch'en, killed Chao Yung-lin, and 200 other persons. The surrender of this missionary was demanded; but the Abbé Mihières said that he had left for Europe; and that there was no means of arranging this case. Hence great anger among the inhabitants of Sze-chuen.

ARTICLE 5.

The passports given to the (French) missionaries who penetrate into the interior ought clearly to bear mention of the province and of the prefecture where they intend to repair. The names and titles of the bearer, and these conditions, that he will not be able clandestinely to betake himself to another province and that the passport is personal, will be equally comprised in this document. The missionary ought not to pass through the Custom House and toll-bar contraband articles of merchandize which are liable to duty. On his arrival at a destination other than that designated in the passport, or if this document has been handed over to a Christian Chinaman with the object of making him pass himself off as a missionary, the said passport shall be cancelled. On the other hand, if it be ascertained that the bearer has gained possession of it by pecuniary payment, or that he has committed some other serious breach of the law, the individual who shall have thus falsely assumed the position of a missionary shall be punished, and the real missionary shall be sent back to his own country. In order that the control may be exercised everywhere, the name of the missionary shall be inserted in the passport, in Chinese characters, which will be taken as proof. The passport shall be cancelled in cases where the titulary should have gone back to his own country, should have died, or should have abandoned missionary work. Passports will not be granted in the provinces where there are rebels, nor even hereafter for those where the Imperial army is operating, — with the evident object of securing loyally the safeguard of the missionaries.

In support of the above scheme the Yamên will recall a missionary case which occurred in Kwei-chow where a certain Chao acted as missionary, albeit his name had no place in the passport register. The Yamên received a letter on this subject from Mr. Interpreter Devéria, in which the latter showed how, according to an old French register, the murdered missionary Chao had received a passport, dated the 2nd day of the 6th month of the 4th year of T'ung-chih, in which he was

called Jui-Lo-ssŭ; that his name of Chao was
erroneous; that the victim was really the said
Jui-Lo-ssŭ; that, on the other hand, the same
Jui-Lo-ssŭ was inserted under number 325 as
going to Sze-chuen and thence to Kwei-chow.
However, the Yamên was able to convince itself that neither this name of Chao nor that of
Jui-Lo-ssŭ figured on its passport register.
There was, therefore, a double mistake in the
name of the missionary and in that of his residence.   How, then, could one establish an
identity and secure to the party interested
efficacious protection?

There was also an affair of murder committed by the missionary Splingaert on the
person of a Russian.   This Splingaert was first
of all a missionary, then entered the Prussian
Legation as constable.   He none the less retained his passport, so that he handed it over
to some one else, or lost it, so that not only
an abuse, in passing as a missionary, occurred,
but grave inconveniences to public affairs might
have arisen in case the said passport had fallen
into the hands of rebels.   On the other hand,
the dignity of missionaries seems to us to be
seriously injured by such irregularities.

ARTICLE 6.

The aim of the missionaries being to exhort men to virtue, it is befitting that before admitting an individual to the privileges of religion, he should be examined as to whether he has undergone any sentence or committed any crime. If this examination be in his favour he may become a Christian ; if the contrary he should not be allowed to become one. One ought, moreover, to act as the ministers of our religion do, who give notice to the inspectors of ten families, and cause the name of the person to be entered in the register with this purpose. In the same way the missionaries ought to give notice to the authorities, who will take note of the day of the month and of the year of admittance, of the country, and of the station in life of the individual, and will ascertain if he has ever undergone any sentence, or if he has ever changed his name. By acting thus all confusion will be avoided. If a Christian should be sent on a mission, and he should die on the way, notice should be given to the proper authority. If, after being converted, a person commits some crime, he should be dismissed, and no longer regarded as belonging to the religion.   Every month, or at least every three months, the authorities ought to be informed of the number of conversions.   The authorities also should act as they do in regard to our temples, that is to say, they should go every month, or at least every three months, to inspect the missions.   This course will do no harm to religion, but, on the contrary, will ensure tranquillity.

In the ninth year of the reign of T'ung Chih, the Government of Kwei-chow gave notice to the Yamên that at Kwei-ting-hsien some people, who were formerly nothing better than thieves, were forming a part of a militia of which the Christians, Yuan Yü-hsiang and Hsia Chen-hsing, were the leaders.   Passing themselves off as Christians, these men were highly thought of; however, they committed all sorts of disturbances, killed Wang Chiang-pao and Tso Yin-shu, seriously wounded three other persons, and carried off from the houses not only money, but also all the objects which they contained, even down to the very cattle.

In the eighth year of the reign of T'ung Chih the Governor of Kwei-chow again warned our Yamên that at Tsun Yi-hsien a petition had been addressed, with the object of declaring that some rebels, of whom the leaders were Sun Yu-shan, T'ang Shen-hsien, T'ang Yuan-shuai, Chien Yuen-shuai, had embraced the Catholic religion, and that they still continued within and without the town to stir up indescribable and countless disturbances and troubles. In the same place, also, some people named Yang Hsi-po, Liu Kai-wen, Ching Hsiao-ming, Ho Wen-chiu, Chao Wen-an had embraced the Catholic religion, and were even employed in the interior of the mission. However, outside they practised all sorts of exactions upon the orphans, and intimidated those who were poor in spirit. They were perpetually to the Yamên, and undertook to regulate the trials. In an affair between a Christian and a countryman, if the mandarin administered justice to the latter, they collected the Christians, invaded the Yamên, and forced the authorities to reverse the sentences. If, in spite of that, the mandarin would not give the

Christian up to them, they returned with the card of a missionary, and claimed on his behalf the liberty of their friend.

Besides, they committed all sorts of attempts upon persons and properties; if resistance was offered them, they struck blows and did not even fear to kill, and were guilty besides of many other crimes.

ARTICLE 7.

The missionaries ought to observe Chinese customs, and to deviate from them in no respect; for instance, they ought not to make use of seals, the use of which is reserved for functionaries alone. It is not allowed them to send despatches to a Yamên, whatever may be their importance. If, however, for an urgent matter it should be absolutely necessary to write, they may do it; but taking good care not to speak of matters beyond the subject, and making use like people belonging to the class of literates, of the Ping-tieh (petition). When the missionaries visit a great mandarin, they must observe the same ceremonies as those exacted from the literates; if they visit a

mandarin of inferior rank, they must also conform to the customary ceremonies. They
must not unceremoniously go into the Yamêns
and bring disorder and confusion into the
affair.

In the sixth year of the reign of T'ung Chih
the Governor of Sze-chuen wrote to us that
the French Bishop, Monseigneur Pinchon,
had, in a letter which he sent to the authorities,
made use of an official seal manufactured by
himself.

In the seventh year of the reign of T'ung
Chih, Monseigneur Faurie,[1] Bishop of Kwei-
chow, handed to the officer charged with the
remission of the letters of the Government, a
despatch to the address of the Yamên to ask
that marks of distinction should be accorded to
a Taoutae called To Wen, and to other persons besides.

In Shan-tung a missionary passed himself
off as Hsiun-fu (Provincial Governor).

In Sze-chuen and Kwei-chow missionaries
took upon themselves to demand the recall of
mandarins who had not arranged their affairs to

[1] Mentioned as Fauré, p. 86.

their satisfaction. So it is not only the authority of simple functionaries that they assume; they claim, further, a power which the Sovereign alone possesses. After such acts how could general indignation fail to be aroused?

Missionaries shall not be allowed to claim, as belonging to the church, the property which it may please them to designate; in this way no difficulty will arise. If the missionaries wish to buy a portion of land on which to build a church, or hire a house in which to take up their residence, they must, before concluding the bargain, go with the real proprietor and make a declaration to the local authority who will examine whether the Fêng-shui presents any obstacle. If the official decides that no inconvenience arises from the Fêng-shui, it will then be necessary to ask the consent of the inhabitants of the place. These two formalities fulfilled, it will be necessary besides, in the text of the contract, to follow the ruling published in the fourth year of the reign of T'ung-chih, that is to say, to declare that the land

belongs with full rights to Chinese Christians.
It will not be allowed in the purchase of properties to make a transfer making use of another
name than that of the real purchaser; it will
also be forbidden to make this transfer in manner contrary to law, following the advice of
dishonest people.

The missionaries residing constantly in
China must strive to inspire confidence, so as
not to excite the discontent and aversion of the
people; but on the contrary to live on good
terms with them without ever exciting suspicion. At this moment there is almost always
discord between the two parties, and the cause
of it is the conduct of the Christians. So as
regards the property of the church, there have
been claims during these last years in all the
provinces, and the missionaries exact the restitution, without troubling themselves as to
whether it wounds the susceptibility of the
people or is injurious to their interests. Besides there are fine houses belonging to the
literates that they claim, and expel the proprietor from them at the shortest notice. But
what is worst, and what wounds the dignity of

the people, is that they often claim as their property Yamêns, places of assembly, temples held in high respect by the literates and the inhabitants of the neighbourhood.

Certainly, in each province are houses which formerly belonged to the Church; but note must be taken of the number of years which have passed since, and it must be remembered that Christians sold these houses, and that they have, perhaps, passed through the hands of several proprietors. It must also be remembered that the house was, perhaps, old and dilapidated when sold, and that the purchaser has, perhaps, incurred great expense in repairs, or has even built a new one. The missionaries take no account of all this, they exact a restitution, and do not even offer the least indemnity. Sometimes they even ask for repairs to be made, or if not, for a sum of money. Such conduct excites the indignation of the people, who look with no favourable eye on the missionaries. Such being the case no friendship can exist.

The facts that are stated in this Memorandum have been chosen as examples among many others to demonstrate what is irregular in the acts of the missionaries, and to prove the impossibility of Christians and non-Christians living harmoniously.

It is urgent, therefore, to seek a remedy for the evil; both one and the other will find it to their advantage, and it will obviate this sole question of the missions becoming fatal to the great interests of peace between China and the West.

We do not attempt to enumerate the many matters which are agitating in the provinces. The object is to separate the tares from the good grain, to punish the wicked in the interest of the good. With respect to commerce, for instance, merchants guilty of dishonesty are severely punished in order to protect the honour of commerce in general. From the time that the missionaries admit every one, without taking care to distinguish between the good and the bad, these last pour into the Christian community, and relying on the support of the missionaries molest people of property and despise the authority of the magistrates. Under these conditions the re-

sentment of the multitude grows deep.   If
the entire Chinese people should, like the
inhabitants of Tientsin, come to detest foreigners, the supreme authority itself could no
longer be able to interpose efficaciously.   Such
are the dangers which the present situation
implies.

The rules which we now propose are the
last expression of our firm will to protect the
missionaries, and have nothing in their import
hostile to them.   If they sincerely endeavour
to conform themselves to them, good harmony
might be maintained; if, on the other hand,
the missionaries consider these same rules in
the light of attempts upon their independence,
or contrary to their rites, they may cease to
preach their religion in China.   The Chinese
government treats its Christian and its non-
Christian subjects on a footing of perfect
equality; that is the evident proof that it is
not opposed to the work of the missions.   In
return, the missionaries, allowing themselves
to be duped by the Christians, do not adhere
faithfully to their duties.   From this state of
things a hatred of the masses must result,

which it will be very difficult to combat, and a general overthrow of order, which will make all protection an impossibility. It would be far better from henceforth to speak the truth frankfully.

APPENDIX III.

❧

SUMMARY OF THE CHING–SHIH–WÊN–SHU–PIEN[1], OR "BLUE BOOKS."

RELIGIOUS PROPAGANDISM: ONE OF THE MOST
IMPORTANT POINTS AS REGARDS INTERCOURSE WITH
FOREIGNERS.

By LI PÊNG-YÜAN.

IT is our opinion that foreign missionaries are in very truth the source whence springs all trouble in China. Foreigners come to China from a distance of several ten thousands of miles and from about ten different countries with only two objects in view, namely trade and religious propagandism. With the former they intend to gradually deprive China of her wealth, and with the latter they likewise seek to steal away the hearts of her people. The ostensible

---

[1] This is the work referred to on pp. 64 and 137, as "King-sz-wen."

226

pretext they put forward is the cultivation of friendly relations; what their hidden purpose is, is unfathomable, but the fact remains that trouble between Christian converts and the common people is for ever cropping up.

Originally the nations of the West had only one religion, that of Christ; but this one religion has now divided itself into three; that of Jesus (Protestants), that of the Lord of Heaven (Roman Catholics), and that known as " Hsila " (Hellenic or Greek Church). The characteristic to these religions of theirs is that whether united or divided, whether in prosperity or in adversity, their missionaries must go abroad throughout the world and endeavour to convert men to their religion and lead them to follow in their path. Now that China has given permission to foreigners to proclaim their doctrines she must according to treaty extend them her protection, but wherever missionaries go they ought to be subject to the local authorities and not mix themselves up with public affairs. It is unfortunately the case that evilly disposed natives of China constantly rely on the protection which their conversion to the

foreign religion affords them, and on the
strength thereof they commit every kind of
base and illegal action. They impose on the
more simple minded of their fellow villagers,
they insult and oppress the orphans and the
weak, they forcibly abduct the wives of others,
they take violent possession of land which is
not their own, they make difficulties about pay-
ing rent due to their landlord, they defiantly
decline in open court to contribute their proportion of legal taxes, they raise a quarrel about
some public matter and then seek to throw the
blame on others, and on account of some private disagreement they go even to the length
of beating and murdering peaceable citizens.
Every sort of crime can be laid to their charge,
and it would be difficult to draw up a complete
list of their transgressions. The missionaries
without sufficient knowledge of the real facts
of the case, and deceived by their *ex parte* statements, are in the habit of coming forward as
their protectors and openly assisting them. It
often happens that they hide away the defendant in a suit in order that he may not appear
in court, and in certain instances when the guilt

of an offender has been conclusively proved
and his punishment decided on, they in the
most public manner have connived at his getting away to a foreign country, with the result
that he is not to be had and the case remains
in abeyance.

Many officials, moreover, induced by a dread
of complications, act from the beginning with
too extreme caution, and in ignorance of foreign laws are glad to compromise a case any-
how.   The result is that justice is never done,
and the people always have a grievance.   Naturally, as causes for complaint accumulate, the
spirit of resentment waxes stronger day by day,
and a desire for revenge is created, which cul-
minates in the destruction of Chapels and the
ill-treatment of missionaries, and feuds between missionary converts and their neighbours
go on increasing.   Although of course the
high authorities concerned take steps to arrange
these matters, they are for the greater part far
removed from the scene of action, and but imperfectly acquainted with the hidden details;
and as it often happens that their respective
laws differ, each holds firmly to his own opin-

ion, and the settlement of the case becomes
more complicated and protracted. They (*i.e.*,
the foreigners), however, are in the habit of
resorting to force, and using all manner of intimidation, press their point, so that even
after the principal offenders have been punished, they claim compensation for the destroyed property, and even after the officials
have lost their posts they, on the strength of
these occurrences, clamour for the opening of
more ports — proceedings contrary to all principles of right and justice, and utterly opposed
to treaty stipulations.

The nature of the situation calls for the
adoption of some satisfactory agreement to be
observed by both sides which will conduce
towards the maintenance of peaceful relations
for the future.

Now, no Chinese subject at all cognizant of
right and justice or in any way imbued with a
spirit of virtue would allow himself to be led
away by these doctrines of theirs. Those who
do become converts are either so actuated by
mercenary motives that they have lost all self-
respect, or are labouring under some hallucina-

tion which they have not been able to throw off; they are either evilly disposed persons who want influence on their side or criminals who seek to escape justice. They must in the first instance have a contempt for law and order ere they would dare to rebel thus against reason and true principles.

Again, although the missionaries are foreigners, their converts still remain Chinese subjects, and a large enough concession forsooth has been made to the spirit of friendliness and toleration in allowing the missionaries to carry on religious propagandism at all, without upholding their converts against the rest of the people. Surely it is not our wish to first force the whole nation to embrace their doctrines and then clap our hand for joy! Such a calamity would be too deep for words.

For the future the name of every convert should be entered on a list held by the local authorities and communicated to the Consul concerned; and each convert should have the two characters "Chiao-min" inserted on his "mên-p'ai," (*i.e.*, the slip of paper on each house door describing the inmates). There should also be some distinction of dress, and if any dispute arise it ought to be decided according to Chinese law by the local authorities, the Consul sitting as assessor. The missionary ought not to be allowed to protect the criminal in any way. Should the defendant prior to his being arraigned not have his name on the list above mentioned he is not to be considered a convert, and will be dealt with by the local authorities as they see fit, the missionary of course in such a case having less than ever to do with the proceedings.

Should any missionary mix himself up with any public matter or resort to intimidation in any way some severe punishment must be meted out to him, and his Minister be immediately requested to have him sent back to his own country "*pour encourager les autres.*"

Printed in the USA
CPSIA information can be obtained
at www.ICGtesting.com
LVHW011024130124
768902LV00055B/2165